11/6/09

To Charlotte,
May you find peace, hope & love throughout these pages.

Sincerely,
Thom Perry

"I trust it will be said of me
there was more done than said."

Joe Perry

More done than said

Stories
of
The Union Mission
Fairmont, West Virginia
1930's - 1970's

"People are more important than policies."
Joe Perry

FRAN PERRY
with FAY PERRY

McClain Printing Company
Parsons, WV 26287
www.mcclainprinting.com

This book is dedicated in loving memory of my father, who taught me "While there is life there is hope."

copyright 2001 by Fran Perry

*First Printing by
WVU Printing Services
1 Fine Arts Drive
Morgantown, WV 26506-6690
Paperback edition - September 2001   *Limited edition

All rights reserved. No part of this publication or its history may be reproduced or transmitted by any means without prior written permission by the author (example) electronic, photocopy, recording, video, film, etc.

Names of people in "Fay's Stories" are fictitious, with the exception of those who have graciously given permission for use of actual names. *Events are nonfiction.*

From "The Sick Man and the Angel" - John Gay is quoted - *"While there is life there is hope, he cried."*
Poet, Journalist, and Humorist Sam Walter Foss is quoted - *"Let me live in a house by the side of the road and be a friend to man."*

Non-exclusive permission granted to use two excerpts from *Mission on Main Street* by Helga Bender Henry - A history of the Los Angeles, California Mission, published 1955, W.A. Wilde Co., rights now held by Baker Book House Company.

This edition of "Fay's Stories" and other Mission history is compiled, and edited by Fran Perry. Front and back cover design - photo restoration, Fran Perry. Cover Photo, Joe Perry

Reprinted 2004
International Standard Book Number 0-87012-727-6
McClain Printing Company
Parsons, WV 26287

franjperry_mission@yahoo.com

The writer wishes to thank Fay Perry for sharing her inspirational life story; Sherri Meek for providing many valuable talents; Mary Leonardi for her continuing encouragement; Vicki Pitts for dedicating her wisdom, patience, and tools; Meg Park for generous editorial advice; Kim Merritt, Georgette Larrouy, Carol Costa and David Fischer for consulting; Judy Muller for reading the manuscript; Janet Shoemaker for editing advice and advocacy, her husband Richard for technical support; and my daughter, Savanna, for her sacrifices during the compilation of this book. May this effort quench her burning desire to know her grandfather.

Introduction

In my father's house was a winding staircase. It was big, dark, and made of a warm, friendly wood I will always know in my senses. That staircase was my window to the world. I used to sit by the hour on the third step from the bottom gazing out the window, watching the world go by. My world wasn't a big city but a small one in Northern West Virginia. When I grew tired of watching people and cars from my window, I'd marvel and observe all the incredible comings and goings in my mother and father's house. I always knew there was never a house quite like this anywhere.

These comings and goings never ceased. People from all walks of life, from all over the country and literally from around the globe came to our house. The big yellow house on the corner of Washington and Jefferson Streets was like a lighthouse or haven. Our port in the storm often became a permanent home for anyone without. Day and night the doorbell and phone rang; the police, the firemen, the rich, the poor were eventually at our door in search of two people, my parents. For some miraculous reason they took in and cared for the wounded and weak no one else wanted or could help.

As I thrived, so did my unorthodox family. People who had not fit in anywhere -- society, their homes, schools or communities -- found a lasting home. Many times my sister and I grew up with more than one hundred people right next door. They were like brothers and sisters, aunts and uncles, regardless of age, creed or color.

My parents' work was called The Union Mission. My father and mother began this humble Mission in 1937, just after the Great Depression. At this time there were many in need, some starving, without homes or hope. There was no work to be found. With the love and support of my mother, father, and their helpers, the lives of people who came to the Mission were forever changed. The unwanted children from our society were at our front door. They had no parents, so I shared mine. Children without shoes got them, families without homes found new ones, men and women whose lives had been ruined found a ray of hope Men from prisons became transformed and had productive lives. The sights and sounds around me were nothing short of miraculous. I daily witnessed people's lives being changed through the power of love. I felt as if my sister and I shared the largest family in the world. We already had an incredible family tree, now we had a whole forest, a few of them like "Forrest Gump."

Long ago I began a mission of my own. My mission is to reach others who, through sharing the experience of my parents' legacy, will desire to help restore the value of human life. To create a brighter world for our youth and disenfranchised neighbor is possible by learning from the incredible history of a foundling Mission that grew to become legendary. It has been said, "one person sharing their history can become the future of another." My vision, inspired by my mother and father, tried and true heroes serves as a blueprint for a new generation of caregivers.

The stories in this unique collection are of true survivors among us who have overcome the greatest of life's tragedies. Humor was the key ingredient in this love story with an unusual twist. "Fay's Stories" provide detailed insight into the lives of many in distress who became filled with laughter and joy, lightheartedness and hope. Through my mother's remembrances and voice, the lives of these incredible and diverse human beings are revealed. My parents devoted their lives to the troubled or those less fortunate in our presence. My father wanted to simply "...*live in a house by the side of the road and be a friend to man.*" At the dawn of 2002, the Union Mission lives on as a monument to the vision of a more compassionate world.

Fran Perry
November 2002

1937 - The Union Rescue Mission opened its doors

"What used to be called the Union Rescue Mission was started in a one-story rented building on Jackson Street [in 1937]. It had the look and smell of poverty. In the 1970's the assessed value of the Union Mission properties was $750,000. *It seems unbelievable and must be one of the most extraordinary success stories of its kind.* Behind it all stands the figure of one man, Joe Perry, a remarkable personage any way you look at him. Buildings aren't his greatest accomplishment. What he will be remembered for is what he has done for the welfare of his fellow man."

Fairmont *Times West Virginian*

The Historic Union Mission
History and Growth

A group of concerned citizens in Fairmont, West Virginia, met in the spring of 1937 to discuss establishing a Mission for local people and those passing through Marion County, without homes and unemployed. One local organization issued meal tickets but no housing was available. The Mission in Charleston, the state capital, was contacted to find a suitable person with experience for the task of creating a new Mission. A founder's day meeting, held May 28, 1937, was the twenty-eighth birthday of Joe Perry, the man recommended for the job. The other topic to be addressed was a place for housing.

Less than a month later, a mass public meeting was held with former Governor John J. Cornwell presiding. Deciding to take on the challenge of establishing a mission, community leaders and church affiliates were elected to organize this endeavor. A storeroom, rented at 111 Jackson Street and $500 raised from the community, enabled the leaders to begin the Mission.

In September of that year, Joe Perry arrived to help establish the Mission. With homemade benches, bunk beds, a borrowed piano, and a will to serve, Joe laid the foundation. While organizing the Mission he provided food and shelter to people arriving at the Mission storefront. In October his new wife, Fay, arrived to help "build the framework."

The first few men who came to the Mission were those with alcohol-abuse problems or without homes or jobs. Joe felt it would be a good idea to collect magazines to resell for scrap paper. This would provide a small income for the Mission, as well as give the men spending money and a feeling of self-worth. Agreeing to pick up unwanted scrap paper, Joe spoke with a few merchants and was given a baling machine. A large room was found in the basement of the Hart Building, a former warehouse on Cleveland Avenue.

The Mission was quickly outgrowing the storefront. Not

only was the Mission first in paper recycling, but lives were also in the recycling process.

Early in 1941 plans were made to purchase the Hart property, which included a frame house and a brick apartment. A large space below the apartment was once used as a livery stable. Additional space was soon rented for services and a "Helping Hand Store" in the old Mountain City Hotel Building.

As the need for housing women and children grew, Joe and the board became interested in property located on the High Level Bridge. Dr. Joseph Maxwell, president of the board of directors, made the down payment. Transactions were completed in 1943. There were four buildings: a large house, two block buildings, and a brick garage. Joe and Fay, moved into the big house on the corner.

The brick building, formerly a Studebaker garage, was later moved to the front of the property on Washington Street to make way for the Mission's first new building, which would be directly beside the historic High Level Bridge. A multipurpose building with a large dining room, larger and better equipped kitchens, a multiuse auditorium and living quarters for women was Joe Perry's vision. With the introduction of a youth program, additional living space was also required for staff members. The Women's Auxiliary, a group of dedicated volunteers, became an integral part of the youth work. They paid the youth director's salary and over the years purchased vehicles for related activities.

During 1948 plans were made for the new building. In the first public appeal to the Fairmont community for funds, Joe arranged to have a large dinner at the Fairmont Hotel. He invited industrial leaders, businessmen and other professionals to attend. A United States Senator was the keynote speaker. After Joe's presentation reviewing the accomplishments of the Mission -- that of providing work to the more or less unemployable, and the acquisition of many buildings -- he told of a new direction in the lives of many. These success stories were the true heart and spirit of the Mission. Community leaders were extremely impressed and gave enthusiastic support. After the meeting one wealthy and powerful man said, "If Joe Perry were in business for himself he would be a millionaire!"

The drive was launched and successfully raised $56,000. Ground was broken for the building with cooperation and partial free labor from contractors. The carpenters and electricians were equally supportive. With their generosity the Mission saved nearly half the cost of building this structure. The "Main Building's" official opening was in 1951. Joe estimated the building and furnishing cost was only $77,000. The bank placed a value of $117,000 on the building alone, a conservative estimate.

Through the years many programs were established. The Mission had not only been self-supporting through gifts, paper recycling and thrift store sales, but also the sale of cordwood became a prosperous venture for the Mission. The idea of having a book store was soon a means of support as well as overnight housing for Korean War inductees. Other programs, which sometimes evolved from a need, were established: jail visitations, a home for unwed mothers, and a shelter for needy or abused families. The Junior Police, one of Joe Perry's early programs, helped many young boys in the area. A boxing ring was placed under the High Level Bridge, where boys were taught sportsmanship and citizenship.

The Union Mission was accepted by the United Fund, an agency established to aid worthy, nonprofit organizations. With this help, income through Joe's industrious ventures, and special gifts, the Mission was able to keep the bills paid.

For many years Joe Perry had the vision of the Mission owning a farm and camp. This vision was realized in the mid-1950's. The Fairmont *Times West Virginian* quoted: *"People, discarded by society and furnishings no longer needed by their owners, have been salvaged and brought together on 111 acres of land considered to be among the most beautiful in Marion County. These 'bits and pieces' comprise seventy five percent of the construction at the farm. The materials used were from a discarded prison*

The Perry house - located where long ago stood the old "Old Rock House." Left - book store, house, chapel (later store), and Friendly Homes. Main Building partially visible behind house, four buildings in rear not shown.

Huge stones from "Rock House" became foundation of "most important landmark in downtown Fairmont".

camp in Lincoln County. An Army barracks from World War two was also dismantled and erected at the farm. Various materials from churches, businesses, theaters, industrial sites, a railroad station and a school were all used in the construction of the many buildings that occupy the place known as 'Mission Farms, County Miracle'."

Other property near the Mission was acquired. The West property was purchased in 1956 and the additional purchase of the nearby Barr property in 1960 enabled the Mission to later build Friendly Homes. In 1968 ground was broken for Friendly Homes, a building for low-income and elderly people. Joe Perry loaned the Mission his life-savings of $12,000. The building was completed in 1969.

A historic building, Fairmont's first courthouse and later a church, was finally added to the ever-expanding Union Mission. Historians revealed that huge rocks used in the foundation of this historic building were unearthed from the legendary "Rock House." The Rock House (discovered by settlers in 1750) dating back over three hundred years, belonged to the first inhabitants of Marion County, American Indians. *The house occupied by the Perry family was on that very location.* The old courthouse was known as the "most historically important landmark in Fairmont." With the addition of this historic church, the entire city block belonged to the Mission. From its early roots in the old storefront, the Mission property and farm grew to an estimated two million enterprise of service and good will.

Farm Dining Lodge with kitchen and two fireplaces seats as many as 135 people.

The Joe & Fay Perry Story
Part One

A native of Charleston, West Virginia, who described himself as the original dropout, readily admitted he was in need of help before he became the helper. At sixteen, Joe Perry ended his formal education at the seventh grade. School was a frustration and a bore to this active, inquisitive, gifted youngster who preferred the woods, the beauty of nature and the public library. Joe loved to read. Due to his inability to perform well in typical classroom situations, he was held back several years. Formal education became even more tiresome and tasteless. Joe educated himself and quenched his thirst for knowledge through books. His avid reading contributed to a skill of nearly instantaneous recall. In his last year of school, Joe became fascinated with printing and worked in this field for several years. Later, working at other jobs, the young man's life took a downward trend with alcohol becoming a way of life, which continued for eight years.

Once, during Joe's years of drinking in Charleston, a woman he met on the street inquired, "Are you the Joe Perry that drinks or the one that plays the fiddle?" Embarrassed, Joe admitted he never played the fiddle! He was working in a cigar store where heavy "moonshining" and gambling were a backroom business and pastime. After a frightening and life-altering experience with alcohol which left him in a temporary state of blindness, Joe came to his senses. He resolved to get his life on track and help others whose lives were ravished and ruined by alcohol.

With restored faith he proposed to dedicate his life for service. In Joe's past he had been ambivalent to things of the spirit; his mother, a former teacher, and father, a harness maker, saw miraculous changes and growth after their son's rock bottom experience. Soon, faith in a power greater than his own will proved to be nothing less than divine intervention.

Joe became interested in Mission work. He knew all too well, from his former life, that those in Missions had dire needs. Joe did fund-raising for a Mission in Charleston, West Virginia. Success at this difficult task enhanced not only his wit, wisdom and charisma, but also his sincere desire to be of service. Joe later worked on the Mission staff in Parkersburg, West Virginia. After less than two years in Mission work he was invited to Fairmont, West Virginia, to become Superintendent of the newly organized Union Mission. Many local and displaced persons wandered the streets in poverty and desperation. These were intolerable conditions to the people of Fairmont, the "Friendly City."

At the founder's day meeting, local leaders discussed the selection of the right man to organize and open the Mission. In September of 1937, Joe Perry reluctantly agreed to accept the position on a temporary basis. He was to be married to Fay Summers the following month. Joe and the Mission men got the building in order. He and the designated cook prepared an apartment for the newlyweds. As the month flew by, Joe not only decided to stay in Fairmont but arrived with his new bride in late October. Their two day honeymoon was spent on a Greyhound bus, followed by a streetcar ride to Fairmont!

Fay Summers, also of Charleston, came from a different background. As a child she liked school, especially art. Fay had many friends in her youth and was a very popular young woman. A recent high school graduate, she found an office job with an insurance company even though work was scarce. In those days college was not an option. An active and energetic young woman, Fay enjoyed outdoor activities with friends. She also was very involved in programs established by the Charleston Mission involving church youth groups. Fay first saw Joe Perry at one of these meetings.

Fay noticed Joe in a room filled with two hundred people. Seven years her senior, he was the guest speaker that evening, outlining the activities and goals of the Mission. Joe and Fay were soon elected president and treasurer of the youth organizational committee. As president, Joe gained Fay's admiration as a leader. There was mutual admiration and a common bond to be of service. It was clear they shared a

Joe Perry "preferred the woods, the beauty of nature, and the public library."

unique gift of love and compassion. In less than two years they were married.

When they arrived after the two day honeymoon, Joe set Fay to work painting signs for the Mission. He liked to tease that piano playing was not one of her best talents. He often remarked that he married Fay because he needed a piano player. He would then add with a grin, "I should have gotten a player-piano!"

Working as administrator, counselor, or friend to one in need -- anyone who came his way, Joe Perry had many outstanding qualities. First and foremost was his unyielding faith. He possessed a sharp wit, a keen sense of humor, and a deep love for all people.

A newspaper article once stated that Joe Perry was considered to be somewhat of a superman. In his quiet manner Joe remarked that he merely "had a super power." He spoke widely in Marion County, effectively telling the Mission story and how it grew from nothing to *something*. Joe was called on to speak in civic clubs, churches, and to many other organizations. He is probably one of the few junior high dropouts who has given commencement addresses and spoken at a Baccalaureate service. He became a role model "without degrees."

Conceiving the ideas and drawing the original sketches, Joe worked with an architect in planning the Mission's two main buildings. A voracious reader all his life, Joe kept a dictionary by his side, and among other books, took one wherever he went. If he heard an unfamiliar word, he stopped to look it up.

Once, due to a lack of hotel space for a basketball tournament, college boys from out of town were "overnighting" at the Mission. One boy left Joe a thank you note when they left the next morning. Joe chuckled when he noticed the short note contained six grammatical or spelling errors!

The undertaking of founding a Mission led the Perrys to eventually encounter thousands of souls in distress. The atmosphere of the Mission was that of a family, not an institution. The Perrys later welcomed two daughters into

"Fay Summers, also of Charleston, came from a very different background." Fay and her dog "Rex."

their home, adding new life and interest. The Mission was a joyful and productive entity unto itself and the entire community. "We don't have much money but we sure have a lot of fun," was another of Joe's famous comments. Joe, totally devoted to his work, *lived* the philosophy to *"...live in a house by the side of the road and be a friend to man."* That was the simplicity of his life.

For many years the Mission progressed quickly and rather smoothly. There were very few times of financial difficulty, yet all was not perfect. Throughout the legendary tenure of the Mission, Joe and Fay endured personal tragedies with illnesses. Regardless of these adversities, Joe's priority was the Mission, and Fay continued to be caretaker, nurturer and mother to all who came her way. Accepting no physical limitations, she learned to be an excellent counselor, seamstress, nurse, cook, and barber. Fay, also a gracious hostess, did "just what needed to be done!" She developed natural artistic gifts for painting portraits, still-life, and scenery. The end result of two young and inexperienced people who took a leap of faith to dedicate their lives to humanity is one of the most remarkable stories of our time. The indomitable spirits of Joe and Fay Perry live on in the hearts of all whose lives they enriched.

To preserve for her family an account of the Mission's rich heritage through its people, Fay recorded these stories in 1986.

Listen carefully and you will hear the warm Southern West Virginia dialect of Fay Perry. Through her words you will learn many lessons of love.

Fay's Stories

Oscar

Of all the men who found a home at the Mission throughout the years, Oscar stayed the longest and was the most unforgettable. He came in March 1938, only about six months after we opened our doors. Oscar had no possessions, was wearing a pair of badly-torn overalls and an old shirt. He had been a wanderer since he was fifteen, having undoubtedly traveled to just about every state. It seems Oscar had joined the Marines and lied about his age. When Oscar couldn't hack it, he just took off. He never went back home because he thought they would pick him up for being A.W.O.L.

Sometime along the way Oscar married and had two children, a boy and girl. After discovering that his wife had been unfaithful, one day Oscar purchased a gun and entered his home by the front door. He found his wife with another man. He would have killed them both, but they went out the back door. Oscar took off wandering again and after that incident seemed to be affected mentally. Mainly, he couldn't concentrate and never had a good job from that time on. Before that Oscar worked for the B&O or another railroad company. After he lived at the Mission for a time, he contacted his mother.

When Oscar decided to go home for a visit, he wanted to impress his folks. He dressed up in some secondhand clothing that was sent to the Mission and really looked nice. Another time he went home on the train and borrowed my husband's suitcase. He said, "I'll take good care of it 'Brother Purry'" (that is how he pronounced Perry). He was to be back a week later. The time came for his arrival and no Oscar. About two days later he came limping in. He explained that he missed his train and walked home! Joe said, "Oscar, why didn't you just wait for the next train?" He said, "Well, I promised I would be back and I didn't want to disappoint you!" He started out walking and had walked from *Youngstown, Ohio, to Fairmont.* His feet were bleeding. I treated them and found him some slippers. He told us that on his long walk home, he spent one night in a country

November 9, 1940 - OSCAR is located above arrow.
TOM HARDY is directly across with glasses and mustache.

home. He said, "That lady said, 'Here, I'll take care of your bag for you.' Then I told that lady 'No you won't, this here is Mr. Purry's suitcase!'"

Oscar could have not been more loyal. He loved our family as his own. He had the habit of kissing our children on their foreheads or one of their hands. This was all right when they were tiny, but after they were older they were not too happy about Oscar's kisses. He didn't look any too clean at times. Oscar also chewed tobacco! After they were still a little older, he refrained from kissing them. He was at times very concerned about my health or Joe's. If one of us had to stay in the hospital, Oscar would be really worried until we came home. Two or three times a day he would inquire with the office or hospital, sometimes becoming a pest.

Oscar loved to ride in the back of our big truck and pick up cardboard to be baled in our baling room. He knew many of the store owners and salespeople, always waving from the back of the truck with a big smile on his face. Oscar never wanted to ride in the cab of the truck. I believe Oscar thought if there was an accident, he wanted to be ready to jump! The manager of a newsstand and bookstore said to Oscar one day, "Here I give you all my old papers and magazines, and Joe Perry is getting rich on it."

Oscar told the man, "Joe Purry hasn't got any more than I have!" In relating the conversation he also said, "I had a notion to *sock* him one!" He just didn't like anyone saying anything untrue or bad about Joe. The man was just kidding no doubt, but Oscar took him seriously. Oscar had hit several people. When angered he swung and thought later. That was the only problem we ever had with Oscar. He once hit the truck driver because he thought the driver was abusing the truck in some way. After Oscar hit people a couple of times, Joe told him he would have to leave if he did that again. He did have to leave twice, but each time Joe let him know he could come back after a month or so. The second time Oscar was asked to leave, he evidently had not fared very well. He had lost a lot of weight. We heard he had been seen walking along the road in another state by someone who knew him.

Oscar was proud. When he came back he told us he had been working at the nearby Grant Town Mine! We let him stay and he behaved from then on. Oscar wrote to his mother each week. As Oscar was not a very good writer he would get someone to write the letters for him. He also didn't contribute much toward the writing! Oscar would start out, "Dear Mother, I am fine, how are you?" then you had to fill in the rest! He liked writing on some First National Bank stationery he picked up from the trash. When Oscar's father died he attended the funeral, bought flowers, and always sent flowers on what Oscar called "Declaration Day," then called Decoration Day. He did the same after his mother died.

While Oscar's mother was living he always wanted to send her something for Christmas. I was his personal shopper and it was rather difficult as I was mostly in the dark as to what she would want or need. Each year, early in December, Oscar would remind me not to forget to buy something for his mother.

One day I wanted a pound of hamburger for myself from the grocery store. I also needed six loaves of bread from the bakery for the Mission's dinner. I sent Oscar for the food and guess what he brought back? A pound of sausage and *one* loaf of bread! I realized then that he had a one track mind.

When we were working on our Main Building the contractors allowed us to use some of our men as helpers. One day Joe sent Oscar to the bailing room with a wheel barrow. The men were working near some steps just the next street below, over an embankment. Oscar was to come right back with the wheel barrow. It would have been easy for Oscar to bring the wheel barrow back up the steps where men were working. Joe waited and waited and after twenty minutes, still no Oscar. It finally dawned on Joe what Oscar had done. Joe went up the street and sure enough there came Oscar with the wheelbarrow. He had gone around the block, wheeling it down Adams Street, the main street, as unconcerned as you please. It was equal to four or five blocks!

When World War II was declared and the draft implemented, Oscar signed up. He really didn't know how old he was as he had forgotten his birth date. We knew Oscar must be older than he thought and should not have signed up, especially after going A.W.O.L. many years before. Joe worried because he knew Oscar could not fit into a regimented life. He wrote to the draft board, telling them about Oscar's mental condition. They had him see a psychiatrist in Clarksburg. It was really funny to hear Oscar tell about the question he was asked. He said, "Brother Purry, that man was *nuts!*" Oscar was excused from the draft.

One morning I was sitting in our little office and Mr. Miller who had a printing shop rushed in. He told me that our men picked up his scrap paper and had picked up an important box of printing which was to be delivered that afternoon. He explained that it was not our men's fault since the box was sitting near the paper to be picked up for baling. There was no way to telephone, so Mr. Miller and I hurried from Jackson Street, up Cleveland Avenue, crossed Adams Street, and as we came nearer the baling room I saw Oscar in the doorway. I started running and called out, "Oscar, stop the baling machine!" Oscar couldn't hear me but could see a man running behind me.

Oscar thought Mr. Miller was *chasing* me and he ran in and grabbed the baler handle! Fortunately, as I came nearer I made it clear to Oscar that I was not being chased. He said later, "I saw that fat man chasing you down the street and you were yelling. I was going to let him *have* it with that baler handle!" Mr. Miller and I were out of breath but relieved to find most of the printing still in good shape.

Oscar was seldom sick. I remember he had the "flu" two or three times in the thirty-five years he was here. It was quite a shock when one of our men called from the baling room one day, telling us they thought Oscar had a heart attack. He died on the back of the truck. That is the way he would like to have gone. Joe was really upset and grieved as Oscar had been like a brother, or possibly more like one of our children.

Someone had given the Mission a cemetery lot on top of a hill, and there Oscar was buried among the more affluent. He would have liked that. His family was notified when he died, but no one came and no one sent flowers. Many others paid their respects: townspeople, friends, the Mission family, and local businessmen who knew and liked him. There were flowers and remembrances for Oscar.

"Oscar thought Mr. Miller was chasing me and he ran in and grabbed the baler handle!"

Tom Hardy

Tom came to the Mission in 1938. He was formerly from Russia, another "displaced person" in need of a home. Tom's last name was Americanized to Hardy. We had no idea how this came about. He was a handsome man with gray hair and wore a generous mustache. This was before beards and mustaches became popular again. Tom became our janitor and liked things to be clean. Men can be careless sometimes and once after Tom saw the men throw things on the floor, he admonished them by saying, "What's the matter, you no have a mother?"

Tom had a black derby and Joe often told him he looked like a U.S. Senator when he was all dressed up wearing the derby and suit. When some local artists wanted to come to our apartment and paint a portrait of one of our men, we chose Tom. We told him to wear his red shirt, but he showed up all dressed up in a white shirt and tie! This did not quite fit the character-type painting the artists wanted to do. I had to explain to him again, and soon he came back in his red flannel shirt with no tie. We all enjoyed painting a picture of Tom. He was quite pleased with the attention.

Joe loved Tom. Tom was wise and had a good sense of humor. He was also generous. When Joe's father died, Tom came to him with fifty dollars, saying "You got big trouble. This is for you." Joe accepted it as a loan and paid him back later. He really didn't need the money but knew Tom wanted to help.

One summer it was very hot and humid. I remarked to Tom that he must be hot and that I wondered if the mustache made him hotter? He said, "No, Missus." He brushed his mustache up and away from his cheek. "See, hole. Same like hole in ground, cover up with ' brush' and no see hole!" The "hole" was referring to his somewhat sunken cheek.

Lawrence

We had only been married for a year or two when we suddenly became the parents of a fifteen year old boy. Lawrence had run away from an orphanage. He rode on a freight train into Grafton, and from there he came to Fairmont. He was dirty, covered with coal dust, and hungry. We took him in and enrolled him in school. He was a likable kid, but there were some problems. He really didn't like taking a bath, just like many other boys. One day Joe timed Lawrence and he was only in the shower for forty-five seconds! Joe told him that he had just set a record.

Lawrence stayed at the Mission for several months and one day he just disappeared. We wondered many times what had happened to him. We later learned that when he was eighteen he had enlisted in the Marines. One day, after he was grown, he stopped in and we immediately recognized it was Lawrence. He still looked very much the same. He told us the reason he left so long ago, was that he had run into his brother and he had persuaded Lawrence to go with him. They went to Spencer, West Virginia, and worked for a farmer. His brother had told him that we probably would send him back to the orphanage, and that is why Lawrence left!

Lawrence later came to see us with a young lady he married. He was out of the Service and was working in the mines at Osage (I believe). His wife was from Fairmont and was a real sweet girl. Lawrence had turned out well. They had two children. We were so saddened a few years later to learn that Lawrence had been killed in a mine accident.

Rose -- A Story of Unbelievable Tragedy -- Yet, A Story of Love and Compassion

I remember Rose as a very young girl who came to the Mission on Jackson Street with her parents and some of her brothers and sisters. Her father was a very nice looking man and her mother an attractive young woman. The parents sometimes sang at our service with the children, using a guitar for accompaniment. The years passed and we still saw them from time to time. Many times it was when tragedy struck.

The family suffered hard times in many ways. John, the father, drank a lot and could only find work at odd jobs most of the time. The children picked blackberries to sell and earned a few dollars at times picking up junk. There were ten children in the beginning. Meg, a baby girl, died at three months with a pneumonia-like disease. We were soon shocked to read in the newspaper of the death of Andy, one of their sons. Andy, only nineteen at the time, was found dead on the railroad track at two thirty in the morning. There was some talk of foul play, but presumably he was killed by a train.

One day the children were playing down by the river. Rose and one of her brothers owned a rowboat. Patty, about fourteen, was supposed to be watching her younger sister and brother. She spied some boys across the river. Patty left her little four year old sister Lydia to watch their baby brother. Patty climbed into the rowboat and rowed across to where the boys were. Little Lydia, thinking her tiny brother could swim, placed him in the river! Bobby drowned and everyone was puzzled how a baby could get into the water and drown when he was too young to walk. Lydia, the terrified four year old, never told anyone she had put the baby in the river.

Years later, when Patty's sister Lydia was around thirteen, she confessed to Rose that she had been the cause of Bobby's death. She was the one who put him in the water and had carried that sense of guilt so many years. Lydia later had a child out of wedlock and almost died with "childbed fever" as it was called then. She had some mental problems after that and was in Weston State Hospital several times.

Another son, Delbert, was only sixteen when he drowned in a tragic accident on the Monongahela River. The rowboat he and Rose owned together was often used to go up and down the river, picking up scrap metal and selling it to a junk dealer. This time Rose remained at home. It was night before Delbert started back. He was in the rowboat with groceries he bought with the money he earned selling junk. He was struck by a coal barge and drowned. The next day, bread and groceries were found floating on the water.

Rose's mother had a heart problem and was only in her forties. By this time she had given birth to ten children and was pregnant with another one at forty-seven! One night, knowing her mother was gravely ill, Rose tried to get in contact with a doctor. Her father, Patty, and Patty's husband came in after they had all been out drinking. Her father wanted Rose to get the guitar so they could sing! Rose became so upset, knowing how sick her mother was. Finally, through a neighbor and the sheriff, a doctor was located. He came to the house to see her mother. By that time she had died. Rose had already shouldered many responsibilities as the children grew up, but now the whole responsibility seemed to rest on her shoulders.

Dave, another brother, took his mother's death very hard. He was a very stubborn boy. Dave had always been good to "mind" his mother and Rose, but not his father. Dave was often abused by him as a result. As we feared, poor Dave, just a beaten boy, became violent and was committed to the mental hospital in Huntington, West Virginia.

Dave died there at age fifteen. We were shocked *again* to learn of another death in the family. Rose's father died when the shack he was living in went up in flames. He was alone at the time. Rose had a difficult time making ends meet with no income except a check from Social Security. Besides the brothers and one sister still at home, there was

Richard, Rose's son, a handsome boy born to her several years before. Richard was near the same age as two of her brothers.

One day, the kids were hungry, crying for food and there was nothing in the house to eat. Finally, Rose could stand it no longer. She took a toy gun belonging to one of the boys and went to the grocery store where she bought much of their food! She told me later what happened next: "I was somewhat angry with the grocery man as I had gone in a week or so before and asked him to let me have two cans of tomato soup, a pound of lunch meat and a loaf of bread. I told him I would pay him when I had the money! The grocer said, 'No, I don't give credit'."

Rose continued., "When I went into the store *this* time, I told him, I want some groceries and I mean business, I'll blow your head off if you don't do it!"

The man said, "Don't shoot me, take what you want!" Rose proceeded to do so and told me the man was so upset and excited he swallowed his tobacco cud! Of course, the grocer thought Rose had a real gun. As an afterthought, Rose also took money from the cash register because she needed cab fare! Since she was well known by the grocer, it wasn't long until the police were at Rose's door and she was arrested. We read about the incident in the paper. Joe immediately went to the sheriff's office telling him that Rose was no criminal and he wanted to help get her out of jail. After the grocery man thought it over, he dropped the charges, especially since it was a toy gun. Joe asked Rose why she hadn't come to see him if she needed food! Her reply was, "Well, Mr. Perry, I hated to bother you so much!" We had helped them from time to time. Still another brother, George, died in a mental hospital. He, along with Rose and some of the others, went berry picking one day when it was extremely hot. On their way home, they stopped at a spring and got some cold water. George drank about three glasses without stopping. He became very ill and Rose was able to get him into the emergency room at Fairmont Hospital. As George seemed to have some mental problems, he was sent from there to St.

Mary's where he appeared to be all right and wanted to come home. Rose had no way of going there to bring him home, so he ran and walked most, if not all the way home. When he arrived home his feet were swollen and blistered and Rose soaked his feet and dressed them. After George was better Rose sent him to school with the other kids. One day, two police officers came to the door and wanted to know where George was, saying they had to take him back to St. Mary's. Rose begged them not to take him, saying that he was OK now, but the police said they had no other alternative as they had orders to pick him up. Rose said, "I got down on my knees and *begged* them not to take him." George was sent to Lakin State Hospital where he died at the age of fourteen. Rose told me he died from shock treatment, for his mental illness.

After the children had grown up, and Rose herself spent time at Weston State Hospital for mental illness, she came to the Mission to live. She received a welfare check and helped our cooks with some of the dish washing. I am sure while she was here that she had more spending money than she had ever had in her life. She made friends here, and two have been special ones. One was Helen, who later became a staff member, and the other was Carol. Rose seemed to be happy here, but Carol wanted to move from the Mission and find a place where she could cook and they would be on their own. Rose liked the idea, so they packed their things and left after finding an apartment on the east side. For a few years things seemed to go very well, but in the past several years Rose and Carol fell on hard times. They did not have heat, water, or groceries, but they always managed with a little help. Helen, our staff nurse, suffered from emphysema and heart disease. Many times Rose would come and stay across the hall from Helen. Rose would get up several times during the night with her. Helen was good to Rose, helping when she and Carol were short of cash.

Through *all* this, Rose never became bitter. She is a compassionate, loving person and a very giving person. When friends or acquaintances have a need she is always there for them.

Footnote: Rose's sister Patty died after a bout with cancer at the age of sixty-two. She waited too long before telling anyone about the lump she found in her breast. Rose was the first to know, but it was too late. Richard, Rose's son, helped his mother from time to time, but also experienced tragedy. He had two children who perished in a fire. This, of course, was another loss for Rose -- her grandchildren.

Dan

Joe and I met Dan in the early days of the Mission, perhaps 1938. His parents died when he was very young, so foster parents reared him. When they died Dan was again without a home, and had been sleeping in a service station on Fairmont Avenue. Dan was a personable young man around twenty years old. At the time we only had two other young men; all the rest of the men were older. One of the young men was Bill. Dan was ambitious and helped with the collection of waste paper until he found a commission job selling pots and pans. A few times he earned a little extra money and bought a quart jar of cherry preserves. Once when Bill generously helped himself, Dan said, "Them preserves are rich Bill, it don't take much to do ya!" We laughed and kidded Dan about this.

While living at the Mission, Dan developed into a fine young man, deeply rooted in family and ideals of the Spirit. Dan truly loved his neighbor as himself. He eventually enlisted in the Army and was stationed in Ohio.

Dan went alone to a church. Since he was early, he was noticed by an usher. After the service, the usher invited Dan to his home for dinner. There he met Anita, the host's daughter, and after a few more visits Dan and Anita were in love. A few months later Dan brought his fiancee for a visit. He wanted us to meet her parents. I'm sure Dan felt like we were his parents.

Anita, his fiancee, was a music teacher and a lovely young lady. She and Dan settled in Ohio when he was discharged from the Army. Over a period of years they were blessed with three or four children. We heard from them from time to time. One of their sons, Frank, was in Rescue Mission work for awhile. Dan once worked for the B&O Railroad. When a settlement was made for a back injury, Dan bought an organ for his church and sent the Mission five hundred dollars.

He later had jobs working in various stores and was made manager of at least two. Dan was a loving family man and I'm sure he made his mark in the world.

The DeLuca Family

Another family we came in contact with was the DeLuca family. When Joe and I first came to Fairmont there were seven children. Soon Joe had a namesake, Joseph DeLuca Jr! The father's middle name was also Joseph. We were able to help this family in many ways during the next several years. Since Mr. DeLuca was not naturalized he wasn't eligible for a job on the W.P.A., a public works project. They received just a few dollars each week from "direct relief." They did well with the little they had.

They were very clean and industrious. Mrs. DeLuca washed clothes for her sister and earned a little money. Occasionally, Mr. DeLuca was able to pick up a few dollars at odd jobs. We took food to the family whenever we had more perishables than the Mission could use. Local stores gave us bread, vegetables and other food they had left over on Saturday nights.

My husband secured a job for Mr. DeLuca as a laborer for a local company. This lasted a year or so. It was a happy day for Mr. DeLuca when he became a U.S. Citizen. It wasn't easy. The first time he failed, because when asked "What *is* the Fourth of July?" Mr. DeLuca thought for a long time then said, "Oh, *I* know, it's July the fourth!" He had to go to school for a time and was able to pass.

He was later employed by the W.P.A and the family did fairly well, except for the time Mrs. DeLuca almost lost the use of her washing machine. Payments were due and there was no money. We had very little ourselves, but Joe paid the thirty-five dollars they owed on the washing machine. Mr. DeLuca was supposed to make small payments to Joe until the money was paid back. After about three payments Joe said he felt bad about taking the money from Mr. DeLuca. Joe told him he didn't owe anymore.

Before long, times were better and Mr. DeLuca secured a job at a local mine. He worked for several years and bought a home. Unfortunately, he was injured and had to quit work. Joe knew someone at a local plant and was able to get a job for Mrs. DeLuca. She worked for many years but finally had to quit because of ill health.

Those early years were wonderful with the DeLuca family. Joe would go in the old car to bring the DeLuca children to the Mission. Joe often remarked that they were very slow in getting ready. He later discovered why. They had only one comb and it took quite a while to comb the hair of seven children! All the girls had really long hair.

We sometimes gave Mrs. DeLuca money to buy ingredients for spaghetti and we joined them for dinner. That was the best spaghetti! I don't know whether that was because of the cook or the family. They were always so happy to have us there. Often Joe had to hold two children at a time on his lap. Little Johnny had a badly infected eye once and no doubt could have lost his sight. Mr. DeLuca called Joe, who took the boy to see Dr. J. M. Maxwell, an ophthalmologist and president of our board of directors. Doctor Maxwell saved Johnny's eyesight.

I was amused with Mrs. DeLuca when our firstborn arrived. The paper made an error and reported that we had a boy. When Mrs. DeLuca came to the hospital and found out differently, she was so disappointed! We were quite happy with a little girl.

The Hawkins Family

Today I visited the funeral home where Emma Hawkins' death was being mourned by her family and friends. I saw all of her children, now in their thirties, forties and fifties. They were very young when Joe and I came to Fairmont. Edna Jean had not been born to Emma when we met. Now a beautiful, mature woman, Edna Jean immediately recognized me. I hadn't seen her since she was in high school.

The funeral brought back a lot of memories of the Hawkins family. They were among the first needy families we visited when we first came to Fairmont. George, the father, worked regularly for the city but was an alcoholic. When he was under the influence he was a tyrant, abusing his wife and family. He often punished his children by not letting them come to summer camp or some other activity we had planned. Once George beat his oldest daughter Ernestine with a strap. It left marks on her back and legs for days. Ernestine later had spinal meningitis and died.

There were eight children in the family. Jacob, the second son, had a wonderful personality but became an alcoholic and spent time in the penitentiary for stealing copper, as I recall. Also, another son named Amos was in trouble on similar charges two or three times when he was younger. They turned out well after all these years. They are good workers and good citizens.

The Lions Club held a huge Christmas party each year for all the Mission children, including the Hawkins and DeLuca children. Two board members' names were also Hawkins and DeLuca. What a ribbing they took when so many Hawkins and DeLuca names were called out!

Another daughter, Tessie, met a boy named David Rowe, who also attended our classes and clubs. They fell in love and were married, moved to Ohio and raised a nice family. Tessie always writes a note on her Christmas card and expresses the good times they had at camp and all the other activities planned for them by the Mission. I expect the most happy memories of early youth the entire family has are the memories connected with the Mission.

George Hawkins, the father, came home from work one time and gave his wife grocery money from his weekly check. He then went out and drank up all that was left. He came home and demanded she give some of the grocery money back. For once, Emma stood up to him. George threatened to jump off the bridge if she didn't give him the money. She refused, not taking him seriously. He did go out and jump off a bridge which was not too far from their home. Unfortunately or fortunately, as one might look at it, George didn't go far enough out onto the bridge and hit the ground not too far from the edge of the water! He broke many bones and was in the hospital for a long time. We visited George, hoping the experience might have shaken him up enough to feel remorse, but no, he was even worse after that.

A few years later George came home drunk and because his wife locked him out, he punched his arm through the glass in the door and cut an artery. George bled to death before he could be taken to the hospital. It is a sad thing to say, but the family fared much better after he died. I am sure, even though they missed their father and loved him, they were much happier after he was gone.

Footnote: The Hawkins visited once during the time of their fiftieth wedding anniversary. Emma said, "The only good memories she had were connected with the mission." She also stated that the *only* present her sister received at Christmas one year was the doll from the annual Lions Club party at the Mission. One brother said, "Us kids never would have made it if it hadn't been for Joe Perry.". He had just retired after thirty years with a major Washington DC newspaper. He left a three hundred dollar check for the Mission.

Joe Corporal

Joe was an ex-coal miner, a tiny man who came from Poland. He needed a place to stay and work. Joe came to the Mission about a month before our oldest daughter, Janet, was born. He loved to work and worked in the baling room sorting paper. "Little Joe" also liked to clear and wash off the tables after meals. If someone started to clear the tables, he became very angry. Other times he would often tap himself on the chest and say, "Me work, all's time, me work."

Now and then he would ask me how old Janet was. I would say "She is fourteen," or what her age was at the time, and Little Joe would say, "Me been this place fourteen years. Me come, Missy no got nothing, Missy bi-i-g!" (holding his hands out from his tummy, indicating how big I was when pregnant). At times he complained about a hernia and was ready to show me if I gave the least encouragement! He would hold his hand over the area and say, "Me sick!"

Little Joe stayed with us a number of years. He had a few relatives in the area. When he died there were more people at his funeral than we usually saw at the funerals of most of our residents. We all missed "Little Joe."

Margie

"Margie" was not her real name. I called her that one day and she liked the name better than her own. The name stuck and everyone called her Margie or shortened it to "Marge." Her uncle brought her to the Mission. She was pregnant and her husband was in the penitentiary in Ohio. She was only three months pregnant and we knew the child probably was not fathered by her husband, but that's what she wanted everyone to believe. She had been staying with her uncle. We thought he might be the father or more likely, a cousin could have gotten her pregnant. Margie tried various organizations for help before coming to us.

She had several brothers and they all had been placed in a home in Wheeling, West Virginia, when her mother and father separated. Her mother was an alcoholic and we saw her many times on the street showing the effects of alcohol. Margie's father was just not financially able to care for the children after the separation. She had one sister who married and lived in Pittsburgh. For a while after Marge was eighteen, she lived there with her sister and brother-in-law. For some reason Margie had to return to Fairmont and live with the uncle, where she became pregnant.

We had no place for her, but Joe arranged for the Department of Welfare to give Margie enough money to cover her rent. We furnished her food and anything else she needed. The room she rented was just up the street from the Mission. I had never been close to anyone who was expecting and it was a learning experience for me. I also knew nothing about labor or delivery. We had a layette ready and I was looking forward to the day the baby would arrive.

Joe and I were out one evening near Margie's time to deliver. I was a little concerned as she had not been feeling too well that afternoon. While we were out, we had her stay at our apartment to be near the telephone. We later stopped and phoned home. The older man living downstairs from our apartment told me he thought she might be starting labor. We rushed home and I didn't wait for Joe to come to a complete stop before I jumped out of the car and ran up the stairs!

Joe called the doctor, who arrived in a short while. The doctor looked around the apartment and was quite interested in my paintings, especially a portrait I had done of Joe. He wondered if I might do a portrait of him sometime! I thought this was all very nice, but I was getting nervous and thinking, why doesn't he hurry up and examine Margie! I thought the baby could come any minute, that's how much I knew. The doctor examined Marge and said we might as well take her to the hospital but the baby probably would not arrive before morning. I was too excited to sleep that night and called about six the next morning. The baby arrived forty-five minutes before I called!

Carolyn was the name Margie chose for her daughter. We loved little Carolyn and I helped Margie care for her. We took pictures of the baby and were as proud as if she were our very own. Soon after Carolyn was born, the Mission bought the Hart property. Joe and I moved into an apartment on the top floor and Marge had the room across the hall. She and Carolyn ate their meals with us and were just like family. Marge was a good worker and helped with all the washing, ironing, and other housework. She was very particular with the care of Carolyn.

Marge ironed her diapers, little shirts and everything! I tried to tell Margie she was doing unnecessary work, but she told me that I would be just as particular when I had a child of my own. She found out better later on! Joe enjoyed the baby and called himself her "Poop deck pappy!" The name was shortened to "Poop deck" and when Carolyn heard his footsteps down the hall she called out "Poo-da, Poo-da!"

The men's dorm and dining room were down a flight of stairs. Marge became acquainted with David Oakes and they fell in love. We tried to discourage the relationship as we thought she didn't know him all that well. Marge and David went to live with her father when Carolyn was two and a half years of age. Marge had been a great help to me, especially when our daughter Janet was born. Carolyn was a year and a half old when Janet arrived. Marge baby-sat for me when I played the piano for our service or had to go shop for groceries. Carolyn was also helpful. The rooms of our apartment were in a straight line. The kitchen was the furthest from Janet's room. Sometimes I could not hear her crying. Since Carolyn was just across the hall she would call out, "Missy, Jangie kying!"

Marge and David later moved to Southern West Virginia and David got a job in a department store. They were married after Marge's divorce from the man imprisoned in Ohio. They seemed very happy for a while and Marge reminded me of our objection when she started dating David. I admitted we were wrong and were happy for them. There were some problems later and Marge left David at least twice and came back to Fairmont, one time staying at the Mission for a while. The trouble seemed to be his strictness with Carolyn. We kept in touch over the years.

Carolyn grew into a lovely young lady. We were surprised one day when they all came for a visit. Marge and David had adopted a little boy. A few years went by and we didn't hear much. One day *Carolyn and David* showed up with three children and said they were married and Marge was living in Pittsburgh! Carolyn admitted that the boy who visited before with them was not adopted by Marge and David, but really was Carolyn and David's son! They later came back in a van belonging to the department store -- all these children came tumbling out! They had six and seemed very happy. David was a proud papa and Carolyn was one of those women born to be a mother. We received Christmas cards from them for several years.

When I thought of this family I couldn't help but think poor Margie, wondering how she felt about Carolyn and David. One afternoon, Edith Closson, one of our cooks, called me from the kitchen saying, "Mrs. Perry, there is a lady here who says she knows you from the early days of the Mission." I couldn't figure out who it might be. Imagine my surprise when I went to the door and there stood Marge. I thought I heard she died, but knew I was seeing the real Marge. She came in and we had a really good visit. Marge said she was living back in Southern West Virginia in an apartment for the elderly. She seemed happy and in good health. She was very ill for several years. Through faith, Marge came to terms with her daughter's relationship with David. Thankful for a deeper, richer spiritual life, Marge found peace through acceptance of Carolyn and David's marriage. She said Carolyn later married for the second time and has ten children, two by her second husband. I would love to see them all someday.

Bob King

Bob came to the Mission when our daughter Janet was only about a month old. He was an alcoholic, which seemed to be his only problem. An easygoing, quiet little man, Bob was very gifted in carpentry and a good maintenance man. As Janet began to walk, he liked to talk to her and buy toys she liked. He bought Janet her very first doll on her first Christmas. He carved a loving cup from her first Christmas tree, making it with spoon handles that were gilded gold.

We used the second floor of our industrial building, located where Everest Drive is now, for a carpentry shop for Bob. He repaired furniture and made things for our Helping Hand Store. I admired a broken-down platform rocker we obtained from a old warehouse near the shop. He fixed up the chair and later found an exact mate to it, except the ornamental top to the back was missing. He carved and copied the other ornament and I was happy to have two beautifully matching antique chairs.

About once a year, or once every two years, Bob left for several weeks and we knew he went away to drink. He had too much respect for us and the Mission to drink here. He always came back with a present for Janet.

Grandma Roten, a former cook, planned to retire when she reached sixty-five years of age. She longed for a little home to share with her daughter Bessie. Her other daughter, Nell, offered enough land near her home for Grandma and Bessie. Joe acquired an old school house located in Coal Run Hollow. Bob King razed it, and moved the lumber to Nell's property. He built a little three room house for Grandma and Bessie. They paid Bob the salary he was making at the Mission, which was four dollars a day. This was in the 1940's and that was considered a fair wage considering room and board were furnished.

One evening near dusk, Bob took Janet for a walk and bought her an ice cream cone. She was around three years old. She noticed the stars were starting to come out in the sky and asked Bob about them. He told her God put the stars there. A few evenings later she didn't see any stars. She remarked to Bob, "Bobby, God forgot to put the stars out tonight, didn't he?"

We trusted Bob completely. When I went grocery shopping each Friday I usually left Janet with Bob in the shop. He kept some toys there for her to play with, and he enjoyed having her company. He was a good baby-sitter.

The last drinking spell for Bob was his downfall. He left the Mission and was staying down on Washington Street. There was a gas heating stove in the room where he slept. The gas was on but not lit when he was found the next morning. We don't know if it was accidental or if he deliberately took his own life. We were heartsick. We loved him so much and he was a wonderful human being. What a waste!

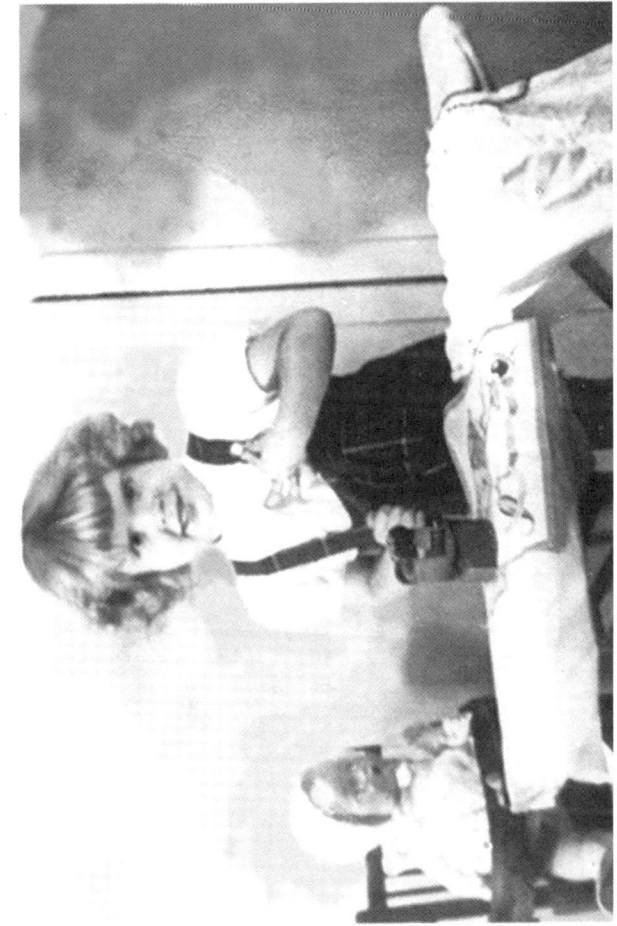

Bob bought Janet her first doll on her first Christmas.

"We used the second floor of our industrial building, located where Everest Drive is now, for a carpentry shop for Bob."

The "Church on Wheels" -
This work of art was built by Joe and the men during the early 1940's.   *Story in Appendix*

Martha Nelson Alkire

Martha Nelson arrived in Fairmont with Frances Hampton on June 15, 1945. Newly graduated and trained in youth work, they traveled by train to West Virginia from upstate New York. These young women came to conduct summer activities for the Mission children. The real reason we invited them was that Joe wanted to see how they would fit in as youth workers on a permanent basis! After the week was over they went back to New York, collected their belongings and returned to plan for our first summer camp. It was clear they were the right ones for the job. Many downtown children, as well as those from mining camps, came to the Mission for fun and fellowship.

In the fall, Martha and Frances started an outreach program in various communities. In a few years they were conducting many youth activities. They traveled deep into mining towns and other locations where there was a physical or spiritual need. Martha and Frances worked well together and adjusted to many situations. There was always a lot of laughter when they practiced their "Mission Musical Messengers" trio with Joe.

They often laughed about the first vehicle they shared with Joe. After a while the roof leaked when it rained. If they went through a puddle, which was often, water came up through the floorboards. Martha held up an umbrella over the roof of the car to keep the rain out but couldn't do much about the other! They were good sports.

On September 23, 1955, Martha married Nimrod (June) Alkire Jr. She continued to work with the youth after their first child, Paul, was born. They lived in one of the houses the Mission owned on Washington Street. After the birth of Rebecca five years later, Martha worked mainly as our part-time bookkeeper. She worked full-time in that capacity after "Becky" was older. When June and Martha first married, because of a seventeen year age difference, we were concerned about their having children. We thought June might not live long enough to raise them. June lived

The "Mission Musical Messengers"
From left to right, Martha Nelson Alkire, Joe Perry, and Frances Hampton.

to see Becky graduate and get her first teaching position. Paul was interested in cooking and took courses to prepare for culinary school. While getting hands-on experience in resorts and restaurants Paul met a well-known chef. Impressed with Paul's enthusiasm and skill, the chef invited him to be his guest at the Culinary Arts Olympics in Germany.

Martha retired in June 1993, making her our longest-serving employee, forty-eight years! Martha shared Joe's deep love and concern for people. She was very kind and compassionate. We also had contact with her mother and brother, Joe Nelson.

Now, Martha lives in an apartment near her daughter in Indiana and is enjoying her grandchildren, James and Timothy. Bless you, Martha. We love and miss you. Paul is a personal chef in Hawaii and in Oregon part of the year. He has lived on Maui for many years.

Footnote: I received a beautiful letter from Paul in the year 2000, expressing his love and remembrances of the Mission. We are still in contact with Martha and her family. Becky also has many fond memories of being a "Mission kid."

Note: (2/24/01) Recently I recalled to Frani the incident about Martha, Frances, Joe and I playing golf. Martha and I were out on the fairway and not knowing that much about golf, I stood right behind her. Martha swung back and broke my nose! We all laughed about that incident for years to come.

Nimrod (June) Alkire

In the 1940's Nimrod Alkire Sr., a retired circuit rider preacher, brought his son "June" to meet us. They both attended our interdenominational services from time to time. June enjoyed visiting and helping with the men, especially the older ones. He started volunteering his services about twice a week. He was glad to shave, bathe or help with any personal needs the older men were unable to do for themselves.

When Friendly Homes opened, June saw the need for someone to look after older or disabled men on a full-time basis. He eventually took an early retirement from the Owens Illinois Plant so he could take over this responsibility. June was wonderful with all the men and everyone appreciated him. He also contributed in other ways. He had quiet talks and prayers in our Men's Building with any of the men who might need a shoulder to lean on, someone to care. June's presence did so much for these men. He had a great gift for counseling with the men. They knew his sincerity of heart was genuine. He also drove our people to appointments or anything asked of him.

June had deeply set, loving eyes, a smile that would warm your heart and a good sense of humor. June couldn't help but snort when Joe made him laugh. Sometimes in the Mission dining room at evening meal time, he laughed so hard at Joe's stories he cried! When June ate too much he started sneezing. I think Joe or someone else nicknamed him Sneezy and Martha, Breezy. My husband, June, and others did jail visitations on Sunday afternoons. In early childhood Frani heard me say to Martha, "Oh, June's up at the jail!" Frani couldn't understand why *June* would be in jail!

June passed on in late spring of 1984. Right up to the very last he gave to all who met him unconditional love and compassion. Testimonies to June's good works live on in the hearts of all those he helped. June was one of a kind!

Men's Building Dorm 1940's - "June enjoyed visiting and helping the men, especially the older ones."

Frances Hampton

Frances was the daughter of homesteaders from the Midwest. Her father Archie was a farmer and her mother Bertha a busy farmer's wife. They had known hard times and were very hard workers. They later moved to New York. Frances and her sister Elizabeth were very joyful children. Deeply rooted in their faith, her parents instilled in Frances a desire to serve the less fortunate and share her many talents, especially with children. Frances liked to sing, play the accordion and had interest in nursing and missionary work.

When she and Martha Nelson came to the Mission to serve as trained youth workers in 1945, we knew they were the "team" to create the programs we had in mind. As the Mission grew, so did the numbers of needy children we came in contact with. Some of these youth came from alcoholic or very poor homes. There were emotional and spiritual needs as well as physical. From the very beginning Frances and Martha brought so much love and joy to the children. They both had ready laughs and fit in so well with the children. Frances, nicknamed "Hampy," loved to hike and do outdoor activities. Freshly graduated from training, with zeal and love in their hearts, they embarked on a long journey that changed the lives of many. They planned and organized many successful activities for thousands of young people over the years.

The Mission children enjoyed our services since there was always something special for them -- quizzes, clubs, "chalk talks" and such. Frances and Martha held summer camps for hundreds of youth, mostly considered to be underprivileged They took the kids on scavenger hunts, had many sporting activities and invited special speakers. Frances and Martha not only worked with the downtown children but also traveled quite a distance to reach the many coal mining communities on the outskirts of Fairmont. They worked from dawn till dusk, inspiring all in their path. I remember some days when Frances prepared for the day. She came to the kitchen for breakfast before daylight, packed

June 12, 1947 - "Some days they traveled from one mining town to another until evening." Back row, l-r (four women): Martha Maxwell (Dr. Maxwell's daughter), ?, Martha Nelson, Frances Hampton.

lunches and loaded all the materials in the car she organized the night before. She and Martha did a lot of preparation for their clubs and classes. Some days they traveled from one mining town to another until evening. They just never stopped.

"Hampy" was always busy at something, later starting mother's clubs and other activities as the popularity of coming to the Mission grew with the children in the community. Many nights our large auditorium was filled with smiling, happy faces of youngsters that otherwise may not have had the experience of putting on plays, singing or pep rallies. Frances was a very special person to all the children and youth. Many looked upon her as a mother and guide. She counseled with thousands of children over the years and stayed in contact with many. Many continued to correspond with her if they moved away, asking for advice as they grew older or just to express their love.

Miss Hampton's abilities in nursing and dealing with people in crisis was also a big part of her work. Many times she and Martha or Joe were called to visit homes in deplorable conditions or to bring the occupants to the Mission. Some of these people lived in hollows that were nearly impossible to drive into. They often had to walk part way to find the people in need. The shacks and run down dwellings people were surviving in were at first, a shock to Frances. I imagine West Virginia seemed like a third-world country to her. Frances and Martha shared many good times in all their endeavors with the youth. The Mission children loved performing throughout the community, especially for the Women's Auxiliary. The Auxiliary, dedicated to Mission volunteer work, organized sales and bazaars to earn money for the youth program.

Footnote: Through the guidance of Frances Hampton and the support of the community, more than thirty young people were provided with college funding. Many of these youth went into nursing, mission, and other service related fields. The offspring of one of Frances and Martha's "kids" was employed with NASA.

Frances kept a daily journal of the events she, Martha, and Joe encountered every day. This was not a journal of the ordinary kind, but one of meticulous and riveting detail. She possessed an extraordinary gift for story telling. Each page of her journal unfolded the lives of people in dire circumstances. The diverse situations Frances handled so skillfully are reflected with deep love and compassion.

In one situation, Joe was notified of a gravely ill woman. After further checking, it was determined she was a member of a prominent local family. The woman had even travelled to Europe in the past, fallen on hard times, and was now living in a rundown house that included chickens living inside! Now, in desperate need and no family to turn to, Frances and Joe were able to get her to a hospital. Many people in urgent need of health care would have otherwise been turned away, had it not been for the Mission.

Frances' love of the Mission and its people was reflected in everything she set out to do. When Fay Perry was hospitalized in Charleston during the early 1950's, Frances kept a special diary. She lovingly recorded the daily events at the Mission so Fay could still feel connected to her beloved Mission family. The diary was sent to Fay.

"Hampy," as she was best known, collected and saved every article ever written about the Mission and all of the youth we had come in contact with. Her remembrances and other Mission stories will be included in the next book about the historic Union Mission.

Marsella

Mrs. Andrew Henry, the wife of one of the Mission's former board members, called about a woman she had known for many years. Her friend was in the Marion County jail. The police picked her up on Water Street, a street noted for being one of the worst places in the city at the time. There was heavy drinking, prostitution and gambling, often resulting in fights and killings. Water Street was a skid row area of cheap saloons where alcoholics and vagrants drank. At that time skid rows were also common in large cities. Marsella, an alcoholic, was drunk at the time of her arrest. The police probably picked her up for her own protection. Mrs. Henry wanted to get Marsella out of jail and bring her to us Joe agreed to bring the woman to the Mission.

After sobering up, Marsella knew she was as far down as she could go. There was no place to go but up. Joe talked to her, counseled and prayed with her and she found faith and hope that there was a different way of life. We had no problems with her at all. Marsella had been married twice. Her first husband was dead and she had one son who lived with his grandmother. At the time her son was probably about fifteen and wanted nothing to do with his mother or stepfather. Marsella's son was ashamed of her. Her new husband, Fred Watson, was also an alcoholic as bad or worse than Marsella. They were separated when we met Marsella.

I spent some time with Marsella and she helped me with sewing. Frances, our youngest daughter, was only about two months old at the time. She developed the croup one evening and Marsella was a great help to me, telling me what I should do for the baby. Our daughter was better the next day. Marsella had been an x-ray technician and wanted to find work. Dr. Maxwell, our first board president, needed a receptionist and was willing to give Marsella a job. She worked for him for some time.

Marsella started seeing Fred again, although we felt she was probably better off without him. We were afraid she might start drinking again if she was with him too much. Marsella was not willing to give up on Fred. They moved to another state to make a fresh start. They went to Ohio and Marsella easily found work in a hospital as an x-ray technician. Before long, Fred got a job with the police department sending out calls. They were very happy and came back to visit eventually.

Marsella told Joe how much she appreciated our help when she needed it. She said, "Joe, everyone else said, 'Marsella, why don't you *straighten up?*' You said, 'Marsella, we want to *help* you!'" Ten years passed from the time Marsella came to us. She and her husband moved to Florida, found work, and bought a little home there.

On a visit to my relatives and friends in Florida, I looked up the Watsons. Marsella's mother was there visiting. Marsella's son was arriving the next day. He was in the service in Texas. It was a joy to see how happy Marsella and Fred were. Marsella left the room to get pictures of their new grandson. I remarked to her mother, "It surely makes me feel good to see Marsella so happy." The mother said, "If you think it makes *you* feel good, how do you think *I* must feel?" I was talking to a very happy mother who, no doubt, had agonized over her daughter during Marsella's years of drinking.

We heard from Marsella from time to time until her death several years later.

Footnote: Marsella was the daughter of a former county clerk and the great-great-granddaughter of a former governor of West Virginia.

Dr. Pruitt

People from all walks of life, schoolteachers, businessmen, doctors, and others, not just the "down-and-outer" came our way for help. One morning about three o'clock the phone rang. It was the doctor who had delivered both our children. It was evident he had been drinking from the sound of his voice, and he wanted Joe to come to his home to talk with him. As soon as Joe could get dressed, he went to his home, a beautiful home, but a home with a lonely man since his wife had left him months before.

Dr. Pruitt told Joe he had driven her away with his drinking and other problems. He wanted help but did not know where to turn. Joe prayed with him and told him that faith in God could help him. Dr. Pruitt didn't know whether he believed in God. He cursed, "This____ scientific mind of mine ____!" After an hour or so Joe poured the doctor a small drink from the bottle by his bedside. He took the bottle when he left and threw it and its contents over the railing of the Fourth Street Bridge on the way home. I remarked, after Joe told me about throwing the bottle, "What would someone think if they saw *you do that* at that time of the morning?"

Joe asked Dr. Pruitt to call again but he never did. When Joe called him a week or so later, Dr. Pruitt acted a little embarrassed and said nothing about Joe seeing him again. Joe was sorry about that; he would liked to have counseled with him when he was sober, having experienced alcoholism and depression himself. After spending time in several hospitals trying to "cure" his alcoholism, Dr. Pruitt died in his late forties, which should have been the prime of his life. What a loss!

Joe Perry - 1940's - "Not just the down-and-outer came our way for help."

"Charlie's Mouse"

In 1987, about a year after I began writing my stories of the Mission people, a copy of a play was mailed to me. The attached note read; *Send to Fay Perry - Found among the writings of Elinor Watson Carroll.* The play was entitled "Charlie's Mouse" and had been written in 1947, ten years after the Mission began. Mrs. Carroll's words took me back to thoughts of Charlie, one of the most vividly remembered characters who came our way.

In 1947 a U. S. Marshall came to see Joe. He inquired about temporary lodging for a man who was about to be released from prison. The man, now eighty-two, had been in and out of prison for fifty years! There were no relatives to take him in and he had no place to go. Joe was reluctant at first, wondering how a "hardened criminal" would fit in with the other men. The Marshall persisted and told Joe it would be just for a few days. He assured Joe that Charlie was not dangerous. In thinking things over, Joe asked the Marshall what the prisoner's crimes were. The Marshall replied, "Our man Charlie made a profession as a counterfeiter!" Joe was rather dismayed at the prospect of a professional in the midst of our other men. Some had been in jail, but usually for intoxication or other less serious offenses. As the Marshall practically pleaded with Joe, he decided we could make some special provision for Charlie. Joe said, "We'll find a room for him by himself and keep an eye on him. I'm sure everything will be fine." The Marshall, now relaxed, smiled and told Joe an interesting story about Charlie when he did time in Moundsville State Prison.

The Marshall said "It seems Governor Cornwell was visiting the prison on official business. Charlie was working in the commissary at the time. When the Governor walked through, Charlie made a little speech, reminded him that 'all that glittered was not gold' and handed him a brand new five dollar gold piece. The Governor was very touched. It was not until after he had gone, the officials discovered that the brass faucets were missing from the commissary's kitchen sink!" Joe really laughed. I walked in and heard most of the story and the Marshall asked what I thought about Charlie's stay. We agreed a room we had used to store furniture could be fixed up. The Marshall told us Charlie would be arriving by bus in three days. We set about preparing for Charlie and wondering what we getting ourselves into. As we talked about his impending arrival, Joc laughed and said, "I'm looking forward to seeing him."

The day of Charlie's arrival came and Joe was waiting for him at the bus station.

He was expecting to see a rather grim, saged felon. No one appeared who answered the description in Joe's mind. The bus was empty and the only passenger standing and waiting was a bent little old man with a cane. The old man pounded his cane and said "Hey, is no one going to meet Charlie? Hey you, young feller, was you lookin' for Charlie?" Joe replied, "I'm Joe Perry. Are you the Charlie I'm looking for? The Marshall must have told you about me. You're going to be our guest for a while." Before Joe could finish another word, Charlie popped up and said, "Am I Charlie? Who'd you think I was, the Easter bunny?" Charlie, pounding his cane like a feudal lord come to claim his domain, shuffled off with Joe. He bragged about how many days he did this time, saying it was twelve hundred. Joe laughed to himself when Charlie said he'd "gotten off for good behavior" and thought, Charlie's going to stop pounding that cane. That'll be first on his behavior list here.

Like many of the "guests" who came to the Mission for a few days, Charlie stayed on. He soon adopted the whole organization as his home. It could never be said that he settled down at the Mission. Instead he tended to unsettle the Mission itself. He wandered in and out, was mainly a fixture in his room and always seemed to have a new scheme on hand.

He liked to take food to his room. We thought he was attracting a mouse or two. That was just the beginning. He borrowed an old typewriter of Joe's and got it all out of whack. He said he was writing a cowboy novel and would be really rich one day. One of his characters in the book was "Hiccoughing Joe." When we weren't momentarily furious with Charlie, we couldn't help but like him. He received five dollars a month for spending money, and liked to buy cokes for us from the police station just up the street. He usually did this when he wanted our forgiveness for something. One day I went into his room and found bread crusts stuck around everywhere. Charlie angrily said, "Don't you bother around my room! You'll scare my mouse away!" "*Your* mouse? I *thought* I heard a mouse in here." Joe walked in. "Judge," as he liked to call Joe, "he's just getting tame!" Charlie said. I told Charlie we could not allow him to keep a mouse in his room. I told Joe I was going to set a trap. Charlie was furious. He said, "Touch my mouse and I'll leave! He's the best friend Charlie ever had and I'm going to go soothe him down now." He walked toward the mouse and got a crust of bread. It wasn't long before the mouse was scurrying over toward Charlie. Joe and I just left the room shaking our heads. Joe said, "Now we're taking care of mice?"

Soon the mouse was also an institution at the Mission. Charlie could be seen lying in bed with his hat over his eyes pretending to be asleep. A few of the men saw the mouse come close to Charlie's face when he was lying down. He had placed some bread near his pillow and had his hat over his eyes. Finally, one day Joe walked by Charlie's room and happened to see him lying down with a piece of cheese between his lips. You couldn't tell if Charlie was awake or asleep. The mouse came creeping up on the bed, reached up and took that piece of cheese from Charlie's mouth!

Charlie worked on his cowboy novel occasionally and announced one day that he'd decided to start making kaleidoscopes. He worked in the baling room sometimes and collected paper scraps and leftover wiring. He said he figured out a way to make kaleidoscopes, using those scraps and some broken mirrors he'd found. There was no telling him *no*, so he launched his project, all the while talking about his novel and the rustlers at "Rainbow Gulch." Soon he told us the kaleidoscopes were not coming along too well. He said the glue was not holding and wondered if he

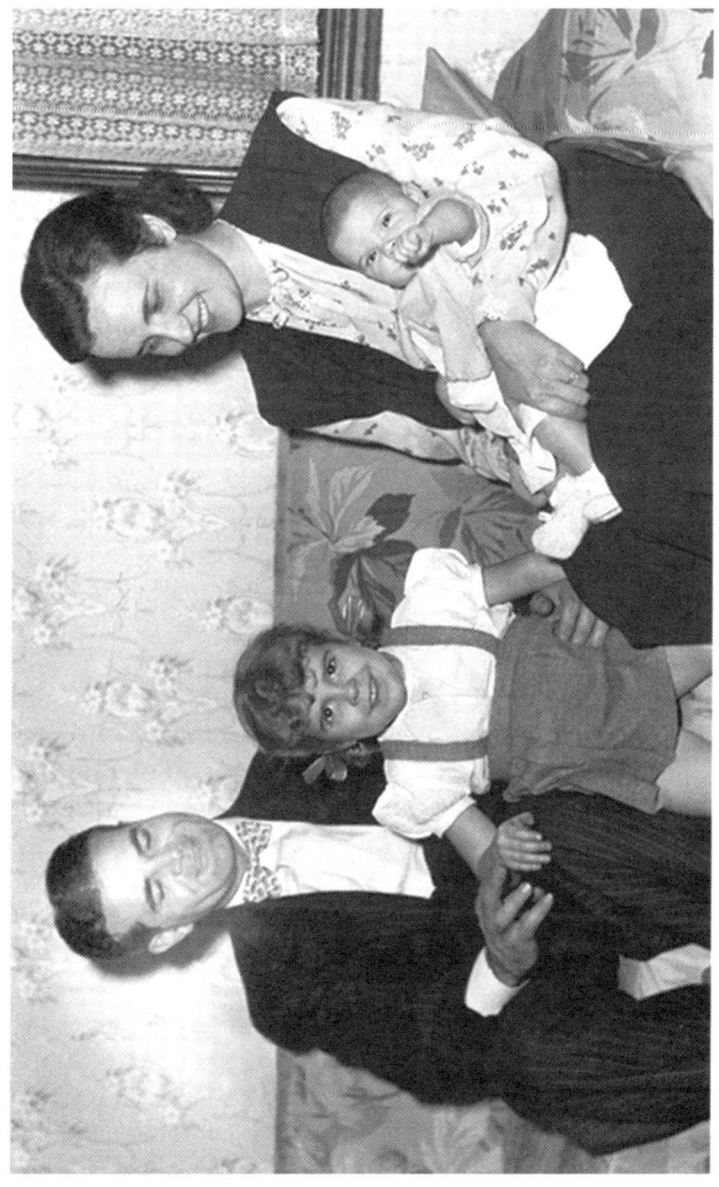

The Perry family - Joe, Janet, Fay and Frances (Joe loved children and bow ties).

could have a "teeny tiny stove" for his room! He said he needed this to make a little solder to use on the kaleidoscopes instead of glue. At first we said no. Charlie made such a fuss, also saying that it was cold in there sometimes and he didn't want his mouse to get pneumonia! We finally said yes, as long as he would be very careful and only use the stove to melt the solder for his kaleidoscopes. Charlie was very content and spent hours in his room with his project. We did see a few really pretty kaleidoscopes and realized things were more peaceful around the Mission since Charlie had something he liked to do. There were fewer occasions he went to the police station for cokes to be used as peace offerings. He seemed to be on his best behavior. Then one day, there was a shadow of a doubt.

A package for Charlie arrived from the drugstore. The delivery boy said Charlie ordered it and had it delivered here. I thought there must be some mistake so I opened the package. It was ten pounds of Epsom salts! I could not imagine what Charlie had ordered that for. Joe couldn't figure it out either. Charlie came in a little later from the baling room. Joe asked why he had gone to the drugstore and ordered that much Epsom salts. Charlie fumed, saying people were telling stories and that he didn't know anything about any Epsom salts. Pounding loudly with his cane, muttering as he went, Charlie walked off and said he knew nothing about any drugstore, never giving us a straight answer. I remarked to Joe, "Charlie is getting to be more of a problem."

One day I was in his room and saw plaster of Paris all over the floor in his room! He said he used this for his kaleidoscopes. Charlie continued to make strange purchases from time to time; a ball of twine, gravy ladle, a bar of laundry soap, waxed paper and a carving knife! He always had an answer for everything and sometimes skirted the issue. If he was questioned too closely he would shut himself in his room with his mouse and sulk. We still wondered about the Epsom salts.

It seemed things were building to a crisis. One day I realized that nearly a dozen spoons had disappeared from the kitchen. Joe said maybe the kitchen helpers had been careless and thrown out the spoons in the garbage. I could understand a few disappearing but not that many. Joe said he'd look into it. Here came Charlie with two cokes and some cookies. He said "Evenin' Judge, have a coke? You take these cookies, Miss." Then something metallic fell on the floor. Joe said "What's that you dropped, Charlie?" Picking up the piece of metal quickly he said, "It ain't nothin' really, just a little piece of brass I picked up in the baling room. Waste not, want not I always say. Found it in some things that came in to the baling room today. Folks are careless." He then wandered off mumbling about a new novel with a character on Wall Street, that "cornered the market, had a yacht and three secretaries first thing you know!"

When we found a few more spoons missing, we decided we had to get some straight answers from Charlie. We felt for some time that something was up. The mystery seemed to solve itself. One day Charlie was at the police station getting one of his "problem-child" gifts of Coca Cola. He put the nickels in the machine but the cokes didn't come out. He pounded with his cane and loudly said "Hey you, officer, come here. Two of Charlie's nickels gone! What do you think of that? Cheating poor old Charlie. Get me my money back!" He told the officer the police station should be ashamed having a machine like that. Officer Oliverio said, "Let me open the machine and see what the problem is. No, it's not empty, plenty of cokes there, maybe there's a nickel stuck. We got a gadget that runs its finger over the coins to see if they're slugs. You didn't put a slug in here, did you Charlie?" "A slug, you think old Charlie put in a slug? I'm honest as the day is long," he retorted. "Well," Oliverio said, "I just asked. Somebody could have slipped you a slug." He opened the coin box. Two nickels were jammed. Nice, bright shiny nickels. The officer exclaimed, "Why look here, this nickel is soft! "Hmmm Government!" fumed Charlie, "Not using good metal anymore. The idea, making soft nickels to cheat the citizens and poor Charlie." The officer confiscated both shiny nickels and gave Charlie two from his own pocket. Charlie was not happy about that. He said, "Hey, them's my nickels!" as officer Oliverio left with Charlie's nickels. Events were building up quickly, ready to crash down on poor Charlie.

The local police called the Marshall, and the Marshall called a secret service agent to investigate. We dreaded the discovery of what Charlie had been up to. A call from the police confirmed our worst fears. Charlie had been making nickels in his room on that hot plate! Under local jurisdiction making pennies was not a federal offense. Counterfeiting nickels and silver was considered a federal offense. We knew Charlie would be on his way back to jail. We were heartbroken, even though he had been such a pain! After searching his room it didn't take long to find the daintiest little mold for a nickel you could imagine. Joe couldn't believe the trouble he'd gone to! It was a craft to Charlie, a work of art, a love with him. We found that the plaster of Paris was used for the mold and the Epsom salts used as a binder! They arrested Charlie. We were so sad the day they took him. He was so likable and to think of a man his age spending the rest of his life in federal prison broke our hearts. Someone took care of Charlie's mouse. A few days went by and we imagined Charlie was in prison already since we hadn't heard. A few days later Joe went to the door. There stood Charlie, pounding with his cane! "It's Charlie come back to look after his mouse!" he announced. A Judge found there was no malice intended in Charlie's act and that justice would be best served by paroling him to the Mission!

Footnote: It was learned that Charlie's first experience in "making his own money" took place in a YMCA!

Fay Perry - 1947   "Someone took care of Charlie's mouse."

Betty Lou

We met Betty Lou through our club meetings at Four States, a small coal mining community outside Fairmont. As a teenager she came to our second summer camp held at the Four-H Camp grounds. She loved being there. When the time came to go home, some kids didn't want to leave and several cried. I remember when Joe and I took some of them home in the station wagon. We came to the place where Betty Lou lived and she got out of the car. We called out our good-byes, but she just ran up the hill crying.

It was a year or so later that she came to Frances Hampton and asked if she could come to the Mission to live. Her mother and father were separated and her brother was the sole support of the family. He thought Betty Lou should get out and get a job. There weren't any jobs available in the mining community and she felt she needed to get away from home. We agreed to let her live here, but I had some reservations as I knew she was inclined to be somewhat temperamental. It really worked out fine and we learned to love Betty Lou as one of the family. Betty Lou was good to come over each day to our house and help me with house work. I was doing sewing at the time to earn some extra money to help pay the bills. I was recovering from surgery and could not do heavy work. After Betty Lou finished her work she would come into the sewing room where we had many nice talks.

She had been a poor student but applied herself in our activities and for the first time developed in many positive ways. Betty Lou had the worst inferiority complex when she came to the Mission. We were so proud when she graduated in the counseling and spiritual leadership field. It was a three day affair. I made dresses for each occasion and we bought her some shoes to go with the dresses. After graduation she was given a position with the Huntington City Mission as matron for unwed mothers. She loved working with the girls, but the position was rather confining for a young woman like Betty Lou. She met a man at the Mission there and they began seeing each other in spite of the disapproval of the superintendent and his wife. The outcome was that Betty Lou left the Mission in Huntington and came back here to live.

We were concerned in learning all this. The more Betty Lou told me about this man the more fearful I became. I thought he was conning her. She had doubts but she really wanted to get married and have a child. She had seen the babies belonging to the girls in the home in Huntington and wanted a baby in the worst way! Her younger sister was married, had a cute little boy and Betty Lou was quite taken with him.

We loved Betty Lou and didn't want her to be hurt, but there seemed to be nothing we could do. At times she would say she wanted to marry the man she met in Huntington. There were other times she admitted she really didn't want to get married, at least to him. A few months later Betty Lou went to stay at her home in Four States. A man came into the Mission inquiring the way to her house in Four States. It was Betty Lou's "friend" and Joe followed him out and wrote down his license number.

Joe checked with the police and sure enough it was a stolen car. It seems Betty Lou's friend had answered an ad for a driver to take a woman back to her home in Ohio. He told the woman he would put the car in the garage for her, but instead he took off for West Virginia! The man talked Betty Lou into leaving with him and said he would marry her on the way. Before this could take place, the state police picked him up. In searching his belongings the police found a picture of a woman and children. We had a hunch the man was already married and we did learn he had served time in a Midwestern penitentiary. Betty Lou was embarrassed about her judgment of trusting the man, more than anything. I think she was really relieved when the situation ended. Later Betty Lou married a young man from her community. She never had any children. We were so saddened when she developed hypertension in her early forties. Betty Lou had a massive stroke and died in the ambulance on the way to the hospital.

Footnote: When Betty Lou lived at the Mission, I took her to Hartley's department store to buy her a pair of shoes. I noticed for some time she seemed to take her shoes off at every opportunity. I could tell when she had her shoes off that her foot was longer than her shoes! Because she had a narrow foot, she tried wearing shoes too short to keep them on her feet! She had been wearing a size seven. Hartley's fitted her with a nine. No wonder her feet hurt. She never owned a pair of shoes that expensive. Later she came to the house and said, "Mrs. Perry, I want you to take those shoes back." I said, "Why? I thought you liked them." She said, "I think they're too expensive, and I don't want the Mission to spend that much money on me!" It wasn't easy to convince her that she must keep them.

Joe Perry holding Francie football style at 4-H Camp.

The Garcia Family

The Garcia family lived on top of a hill overlooking Fairmont. There were many children, possibly eight. The father, of Mexican descent, was a willing worker, but jobs were scarce in those days and he liked to drink. The family lived in a small two room shack. When there was a need in the family, Mrs. Garcia knew we would try to help.

One time it was to take one son to the doctor when he had strep throat. Another time it was Mrs. Garcia who needed help. One of the boys was playing "mumblety-peg" with a knife, and just to tease her tried to see how close he could get to her bare feet. He got a little too close and cut his mother's foot. It was badly infected and Joe took her to an old doctor's office, a doctor (we realized later) who should have retired earlier! The doctor punched around a little on her foot, didn't even take her temperature, gave her some aspirin and sent her home.

Joe wasn't about to take Mrs. Garcia back to that shack as sick as she was and the way her foot looked to him. He brought her home for me to care for and made plans for her to be admitted to the hospital. I took her temperature and it was one hundred four degrees. I put Mrs. Garcia in our guest room and cared for her until the next day. After seeing the sheriff, Joe was able to get her admitted to the hospital, where she stayed for two weeks. She almost died from the infection.

One of the Garcia's daughters had a baby out of wedlock. The baby died in just a few days. They did not plan a service but several friends gathered at the funeral home. Mrs. Garcia asked Joe if he could hold a funeral service for the baby. Joe told her he *had* to take one of our workers to the airport so she could go to New York for her brother's wedding. Joe thought perhaps I could hold the funeral in his place! I was not really surprised at his request. I quickly found Joe's handbook and was ready in about twenty minutes. I went to the funeral home, played the piano, sang an appropriate song, read from the handbook and prayed. I had just finished conducting my first and last funeral ser-

Janet and Frances - "I thought I had all I could handle."

vice! I said one time that I had done everything around the Mission except conduct a funeral and drive a truck. Now there was only the truck to drive! So far, I did not learn to drive for two reasons, there was always someone to drive me places and I knew if I could drive I would get into more work. I thought I had all I could handle.

Janet, Fay and Francie, one Easter. Note the Perry House in the background, right, and other Mission property on left.

1950's - Fay Perry
The Substitute Mother

"Substitute Mother"

Just before our service started one night a call came from the city police. They were incarcerating a young woman for drunkenness and her small child was at the jail. The police station was only two and a half blocks away. A few minutes after the service started, I was playing the piano and happened to glance around. There came Joe carrying a nine month old baby boy! The blanket was almost dragging the floor and the baby was not happy. My piano playing stopped immediately.

I took the child from Joe, carried him downstairs and tried to quiet him down. Needless to say, they sang without the piano that night. The crying child was competing with Joe as he spoke! It took quite a while to get the little fellow to stop crying.

It was no easy job to get the baby cleaned up. He had not only wet and soiled his diaper, but also was in that condition so long the entire mess dried on his skin. A good bath and something used for a diaper did the trick. As there was no place else for the baby, we took him to our apartment and he slept with us that night. The next day the father came for the baby boy and we never saw him again

****

The parents of a little three year old were jailed. They were drunk and had been in an auto accident. The police brought us the crying child who "wanted mommy!" I comforted the child as best I could and said, "You're a nice little boy." The child informed me "I not boy, I *goil.*" She was barefoot so I carried her around most of the time. It was very cool outside and the floors were cold. Her parents were released the next morning, but they did not come for the child until later that afternoon. We were relieved because we thought we might have the little girl permanently.

****

****

Christmas was just a few days away. The police called Joe in the early hours of the morning. Someone had called about three children who were being neglected. Their parents were out drinking somewhere. The police picked the parents up and placed them in jail, but needed someone to care for the children. They brought the Tucker children to us: an eight year old boy, a six year old girl and a baby boy less than two. Our truck driver and his wife cared for the baby and we took in the other two.

When I saw that the children would be with us for Christmas, I knew I needed to go shopping. We had toys at the Mission to give out to needy families, so I knew I could find plenty of toys for the little ones. Then I thought of all the packages my two daughters would be opening on Christmas. I found time to go to Murphy's dime store and bought the Tucker children some nice clothing.

All day long I had been running up and down steps. Up to the attic for clothing to give the needy and down to the basement for toys. By the time I had dinner ready that evening I was *exhausted!* I thought to myself, I'll never make it! I have enough to do to keep me busy until at least eleven o'clock tonight. I was so tired at dinner, my fork was almost too heavy to lift and I was too tired to eat. I was wise enough to realize I had to rest a little. I lay down on the sofa and hardly moved an eyelash for about forty-five minutes and that revived me.

I spent the rest of the evening seeing that the children were bathed, in bed and going to the attic and other places to get the gifts I'd hidden. I still needed to place the presents under the tree. Also, there were things to do toward the Christmas dinner preparations for all the Mission people. I had my second wind and made it!

There were four happy kids the next morning, including Janet and Francie. I gave them oranges, doughnuts and cocoa in bed before they were allowed downstairs! The Tucker children had a very nice Christmas and if they missed their parents, they showed no signs of it. I don't think they wanted to leave the Mission when they were placed in a foster home. We never knew if their parents ever were able to get them back.

Runaways

A Native American boy of fourteen or fifteen was brought to the Mission one day. The boy was from the state of Washington. He was tired and dirty. He said he had climbed into a freight car and was not able to get out until it pulled into Grafton, West Virginia! He must have been in there at least four days and was one thankful boy to get out of that freight car for food and water. We were able to contact his parents and they sent the fare so he could go back home. We packed a lunch for the boy and gave him a small amount of money. He was happy to be a paying passenger this time.

****

A thirteen year old girl was brought to the Mission. She had decided to run away from home. I can't remember the reason, but I know she did not want to be sent back. Naturally, we knew she must go back home. I did a pencil portrait of her and she was so proud of it she wanted to go home so she could show the picture to her teacher.

****

A sixteen year old boy, Johnnie, came to the Mission from an orphanage in Clarksburg, West Virginia. It was summer time and he enjoyed going to the Mission's Farm each day with the men to work. When Joe had time, he took Johnnie back to the home he had run away from. The Sister in charge thought it was all right if he wanted to stay at the Mission. She said, "He is too interested in girls and likes looking at them." Joe said to the Sister, "I'm about forty years old and I like to look at pretty girls too!"

Johnnie lived at the Mission for several months and we had no problems with him. He was very happy and liked his new home. Christmas came and I asked Johnnie if he would like to help trim the tree in our house. He was happy to help. We really enjoyed having Johnnie around.

His Mother finally came for a visit and told her story.

Her husband drank and abused her. She put the children in the Clarksburg orphanage so she could go to work. His mother contributed to their support there and visited regularly. She met a man and decided to marry him after Johnnie came to the Mission. She and the man soon moved to Missouri. Not wanting to spring a family of four on him all at once, she thought it would be a good idea to tell the man about Johnnie since he was separated from the other children already. In time, Johnnie's mother and her husband asked Johnnie to come and live with them. He had a little trouble making up his mind, but finally decided to go if she promised to change her ways, especially to quit smoking!

We heard from Johnnie from time to time; then several years went by and we didn't hear from him. One day Joe went to the door and there stood a young man in his early thirties. He said, "How about a job at the Farm?" then grinned. Joe recognized that smile and immediately called him by name. We were happy to see Johnnie after so many years had gone by and learn about the events in his life.

He told us that his mother was able to get all the children back together and things turned out well for everyone. He was married and had two boys of his own. Johnnie said he wished he could bring them to Mission Farm's camp sometime. He said he would never forget the time he spent there.

Unwed Mothers --
A Home Away From Home

    The mother of a girl from Grafton, West Virginia, came to see Joe about her daughter coming to the Mission. The young girl was pregnant and was to stay until she had her baby. She would be here just as soon as school was out in May. The baby was due in early fall. The girl's family wanted to adopt the baby and raise the child as their own. Of course, Ida, the young girl, agreed to this.
    Ida was a very sweet girl and presented no problems for us whatsoever. She was one of the nicest girls we ever had. You could tell she was from a loving family. The mother was very supportive and visited Ida often.
    When it was almost time for her to deliver, Ida's mother asked us to attempt to find someone who would keep the baby for a month. She did not want to take Ida and the baby home at the same time, because people would be suspicious. I tried to find a home for the baby just for the month but was not successful, so I decided to keep her myself! Ida did have a lovely baby girl. I moved into a spare room with her so I could hear if she cried at night (I had trouble with deafness). I kept the baby for less than two weeks. They got too anxious and couldn't wait to take her home!
    It evidently all worked out well. I heard from the mother a few years later and learned that Ida had married and started a family of her own. The mother still had the little girl.

****

We had only one black unwed mother, Diane. Her parents thought it best for her to have the baby away from home because there were younger siblings. I suppose they wanted to protect the children from being taunted by their peers. They planned to adopt the baby once the young girl delivered.
    After the baby was born, Diane went to New York to

work. Baby "Lily" grew up to be a beautiful young lady and much loved by her parents, who were really her grandparents. Her biological mother sent Christmas cards for several years and enclosed a picture of little Lily at least once. She was thankful for our help during her time of need and didn't mind staying away from home. We tried to give her "A Home Away From Home."

Footnote: These are merely two out of many instances where we cared for unwed mothers. Most of these experiences were positive, rewarding ones.

Polish John

A lady from Farmington, a small community just outside Fairmont, called Joe about a man who had been living in a *hen house*. He needed a place to stay and work. He was a displaced person after World War II and someone had agreed to be responsible for him, but evidently did not follow through. John was a native of Poland.

John came to the Mission understanding very little English and speaking less. Our daughters were young then but attempted to teach him some English, often using their coloring books! He worked in our baling room and was a hard worker. In time he was given the job of running the baler. His was nearly the best paying job we could give our men in the industrial department. John earned six dollars each day, a good wage for that time, plus his room and board. He did well and was liked by everyone. He was a very strong man and never shirked doing anything he could to help.

In his late forties John developed a heart condition and after a while was unable to work full-time. During these years he had been living at the home of a local woman, also from Poland. He was on his way to work at the Mission one day and dropped dead on the street.

At the funeral home John's friend told us how much he appreciated the Mission and said he especially liked our daughter, Francie. He liked her friendly ways, saying she *always* waved and spoke when she saw him. The woman said John talked about Francie a lot. How little we know how much even a small gesture of friendliness means to those less fortunate, older or those just in need of a kind word.

In Loving Memory of "Polish John"

..."he especially liked our daughter, Francie. He liked her friendly ways."

Mary

Early in 1950 we first learned of Mary. Joe and his assistant went to her apartment after someone called about her condition. It seemed Mary was an alcoholic, about to lose her apartment and possibly her job. A month or so later she was brought to our house visibly "under the influence." In order to have some privacy, Frances Hampton and I helped her into the guest room of the house where Joe, our two children and I lived. Mary was still too much under the influence to deal with effectively. After she returned to her apartment, Joe and his assistant visited with her. This time she was more concerned about saving her job and apartment.

Before long we learned Mary was in the Marion County jail. Not long after that, she came to the Mission and told Joe she didn't care about the job or the apartment, she just wanted help in any way. She realized that spiritual guidance and the desire to help herself presented hope in dealing with her alcohol problem. After counseling Mary for a short time, she was ready to deal with her drinking problem. Joe soon invited her to come to the Mission to stay, at least for while.

Joe talked to the personnel director where she worked and got Mary a leave of absence. We sold some furniture for her in our Helping Hand Store and stored her bedroom furniture and personal belongings at the Mission. Mary moved into our guest room since there was no other place for her until our Main Building would be completed in about four months. I was having a problem with ulcerative colitis at the time and an acute type of arthritis resulting from colitis. About a month later the children and I went to my folks in Charleston for a visit. I took the girls down to leave them with my mother for a few weeks or until I was better.

Instead, my condition became more serious, and I was placed in the hospital to see if anything could be done; instead I remained in the hospital for seven weeks and recuperated at my mother's for a few weeks longer. My health

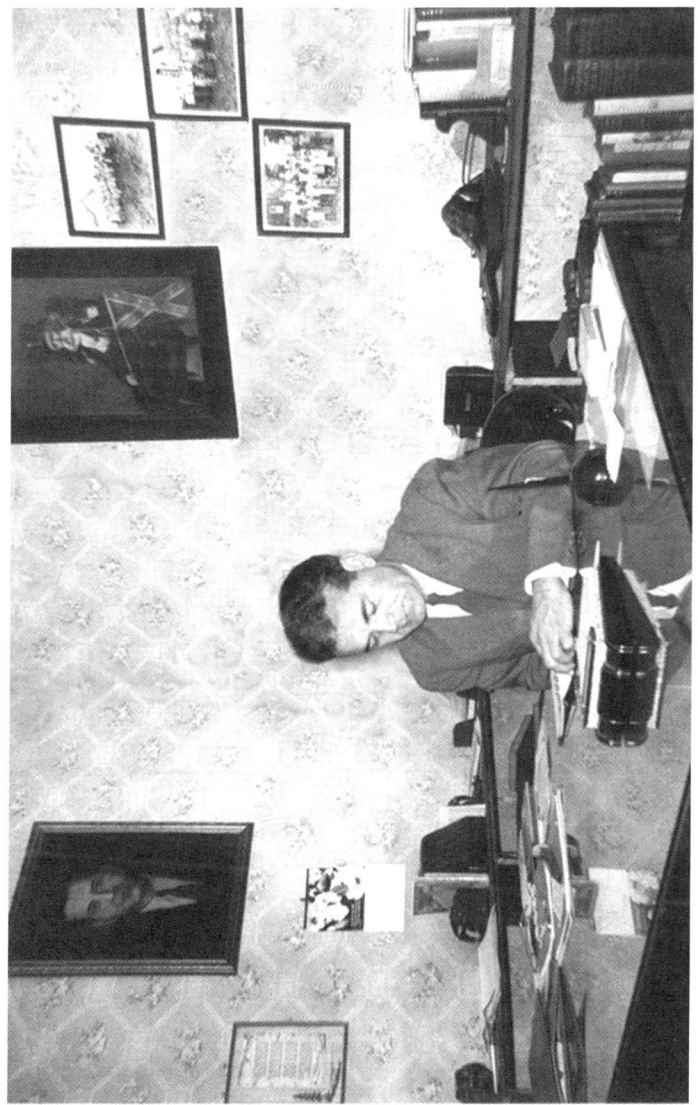

Joe's office was located in the Perry's house until completion of the Main Building. Portrait of Joe (by Fay) above left, picture of Joe's grandfather "Flintlock" on right. Brief history of "Flintlock" in Appendix

was very critical for a time. Everyone at the Mission was praying for my recovery.

While I was away, Mary took over some of my responsibilities, such as preparing lunch for our women workers and doing housework. When it was near the time for her leave of absence to be over, Joe talked to Mary about her future plans. She expressed a desire to stay on at the Mission.

Joe told her he realized that in six years she could retire from her job and would be giving up benefits if she left. He told her that if she wanted to stay on at the Mission she would have a nice room in the new building and he would hire her as his secretary. She chose to stay on at the Mission, and it really seemed to be the right decision.

Mary was happy in her work and if she was ever tempted to drink, we never knew it. We learned to love her, and she loved us as well as the other staff members. We never asked questions, but as time went on Mary shared a few details of her life with us. She and her husband both had been on drugs. She went to an institution for a cure. Mary did not go back to drugs, but later turned to alcohol after her husband took his own life. Mary's husband, who was a prominent physician, had not only been addicted to drugs but also had started dealing in drugs. He was afraid of the consequences and decided to end it all. His suicide had a devastating effect on Mary.

She went back to work and had the responsibility of raising a sickly son. Joe, Mary's son, had been subject to asthma attacks since early childhood. He was somewhat immature and caused her a lot of anxiety. Joe later became an alcoholic. We tried to help him in years to come. He did have two long periods of sobriety, a six year period and later a period of nine years. Mary had a sister who was an invalid, and Mary mentioned several times she hoped nothing like that would happen to her. Mary worked and lived at the Mission for four years and during her fourth year developed angina. Without saying a word to anyone, Mary took a cab to the hospital two different times when she was having an attack of angina. We were concerned for Mary.

The Main Building opened its doors in 1951 -
The High Level Bridge, partly shown left, was renovated for 23.5 million dollars. (Completed in 2000.)

(Note close proximity of Perry house on right.)

We told her we wanted a key to her room, and that she was to call us if anything similar happened again.

Mary loved her work and loved working with the people who came to us for help. There were times she helped me when I needed some treatments at home due to the colitis. This was something many "lay persons" would shun doing, but she was so willing and seemed to be glad to help. She was always anxious to help, but it was hard for her to accept special favors. I gave her permanents and sewed for her. She always tried to pay me and when I wouldn't accept money, she would buy me a slip or some other item. It was frustrating, as I was so glad to have an opportunity to do something for her. She was working just a half day since her heart problem arose.

Many times she would skip the evening meal and snack in her room. We thought nothing of it when she didn't come for supper one evening. We sent her breakfast up the next morning and there was no response when someone knocked on her door. Frances Hampton called me and said she was worried. I found the door key and opened her door with much trepidation. Mary was slumped on the old fashioned day bed, the newspaper on her lap and a pencil in her hand. She had been working the crossword puzzle in the evening paper. What an easy way to go. We could not grieve for her but did for ourselves. We would miss her so. Mary's son Joe was in the county jail for drunkenness when she died. We had to leave him in there until the day of the funeral. We were afraid he would start drinking if we arranged for an earlier release.

There is a lovely lodge at Mission Farms dedicated in her memory. Mary purchased the first building for the Farm, an old Army barracks from Fairmont State College. The barracks had been used for housing some of their married students and families. Prior to that it was an Army barracks used in World War II. We used the barracks for at least twenty years as a multipurpose building, dormitory for girls, a snack bar and a small meeting room. At first, one section of it was even used as living quarters for the Hamptons, our Farm supervisors, until their house was remodeled. Joe kidded Mary and told her we would have to name the barracks after her. She replied "I would like a little better building than the barracks to carry my name!"

Joe told Mary that someday we would build a nice lodge out there and it would be named in her honor. Joe lived just long enough to see the building completed. A letter he wrote was read at the dedication. Even though he was unable to attend, another dream had been realized. Many children and young people have enjoyed the facilities of this beautiful Lodge.

The Mary Fleming Lodge - "There is a lovely lodge at Mission Farms dedicated in her memory."

Irene and Betty

When there was a fire in Fairmont or the surrounding area, we often took in families who were without a place to stay. The largest was a family of ten. The mother had three children by her first husband: Irene, Betty and a brother. She remarried after her husband died and with her present husband had five more little ones! They all lived at the Mission until a home was found for them.

A few years passed and one day Irene and Betty arrived at our door and wanted to know if they could come to the Mission to live. Their stepfather had put them out. They were dressed in jeans and a shirt and brought an extra outfit. That is all they had. We let them stay and Joe talked to a juvenile officer and made arrangements so they could remain at the Mission. Their stepfather could not force them to come home after he cooled off. We knew he would want Irene back as she had the responsibility of looking after the younger ones and did most of the housework.

We also learned that the girls' stepfather would not allow them to go to school. He wanted them at home to work. He saw no sense in a girl getting an education! I think Betty was sixteen and Irene was seventeen. They really wanted to finish school, so we made arrangements for them to finish in Fairmont. One of Irene's teachers, Jenny Harshbarger, was interested in seeing just what the Mission was like, so she came down to check! We were thankful for teachers like Jenny who were that concerned. Jenny later became a member of our Women's Auxiliary and later came here to live after Friendly Homes was opened.

We were overnighting the many young men going into the service in 1950 and 1951. This was during the time of the Korean War. The girls really enjoyed staying here along with Betty Lou Anderson and Sandra Hoult. Irene and Betty worked evenings in the Mission dining room. They were also given their room and board and an allowance each week. They were all good little workers, but sometimes Betty would get a little contrary. There was one time she was "acting up" and Joe said, "Come here, Betty, I want to talk to you." She replied, "I've already been talked to!"

"Who talked to you Betty?" inquired Joe. "Miss Hampton and the Lord!" she replied! Joe couldn't help but smile at Betty's answer and she really was better for quite some time.

There was a young man, Lynn, who was employed by the Department of Highways. They were working on the High Level Bridge adjacent to the Mission. He began talking to Irene and soon they were dating. Irene had never dated before and we were concerned about her. We soon leaned that Lynn was married and his wife did not want to give him a divorce. Irene started staying out after hours. The girls had to be in by a certain time. I talked to her several times, and told her we just couldn't allow that. We were really concerned for her welfare as we did not know Lynn and were afraid he would take advantage of a naive girl.

After a while I realized my talks with Irene were not getting results, so I told Joe it was up to him to decide what to do. He gave her an ultimatum and the result was she left the next day to go home to stay. I was heartbroken and shed a few tears, knowing things might not go too well with her. It wasn't long until we learned that Irene was pregnant. She and Lynn were living together and his wife still had not divorced him.

After the baby came, Miss Hampton and I took gifts and visited Irene in their little apartment. They were married in due time and had several more children. Irene and Lynn have been happy together. Even though they have had some health problems, they still work and are now grandparents. Irene writes at Christmas and sends pictures. We were so happy that everything turned out well for Irene and her family.

The Johnstons

It was in the early fifties when Joe learned that a black family living on Washington Street needed some help. My husband knew the father had died. The man was drinking heavily, fell from the front porch and broke his neck. The children came to our classes and summer camp. Joe gave some work to Mrs. Johnston to help the family. We knew two of the older children best, Gerard and Annie. They seemed interested in having a rich spiritual life. At the Mission's spring banquet we honored our high school graduates. Annie won the award from the scholarship fund we set up. She used the scholarship money when she entered nurses training that fall. I remember the day she went to work on the hospital floor for the first time, as I was her first patient!

Not too long after Annie graduated she was married and moved to the Midwest to work. We were always glad to see her when she came home for a visit. Through the years, we lost track of Gerard. About a year ago, Jo Cottril, our faithful Book Store worker, told me a young man had been in buying supplies and asking about us. I was very happy to learn it was Gerard and that he was a minister in Kentucky!

Playground, picnic area enjoyed by hundreds of youth at Mission Farm and Camp.

The Arnolds: Young Parents with a Problem

There was a young couple living in a out-of-the-way place in the Mannington area. They had two children, one was a three month old girl who weighed less than eight pounds. The baby could not keep her formula down. Being young and inexperienced, the parents didn't know what to do. They were living in a house with few conveniences and doing the best they could under the circumstances.

Someone notified the Department of Human Services and through that contact the baby was taken to Fairmont General Hospital. The young couple was sent to us. They wanted to be near the hospital so they could see their daughter each day. They spent the entire day there. The couple was given a room in our Family Shelter, which was close to the hospital. We knew they were very concerned about their baby.

It was some time before the baby started to gain even a few ounces as different formulas were tried. The baby was sent from Fairmont to West Virginia University Hospital. The Arnolds spent the night at the hospital while she was there. After going back to Fairmont General, a different formula finally agreed with the child. The Arnold's baby gained a few ounces and the doctor told the parents they could take her home when she weighed nine pounds!

It was a month after they came here before they were finally able to take the little one home. It was a happy couple who brought the baby over to the Mission dining room to show the cooks. They said, "You have been so nice to us, and for all the good meals we have had here, we thought the least we could do was to bring the baby over for you to see." All the cooks talked about what a beautiful baby she was. The Arnolds reported that the formula for the baby was going to cost thirteen dollars for eight ounces! An organization had been found to furnish the formula for her. We were wishing them the best.

Lucy

We had the opportunity to touch the lives of many children and youth. Throughout the years the clubs and camps held were a source of socializing, learning and opportunity for spiritual growth. For many children, these meetings and play-times were the joy of their lives.

One of these youths was Lucy. She and her sisters, Rebecca and Glenda, seemed to enjoy all these activities and faithfully attended. Lucy was bright, fun-loving and intensely interested in spiritual growth. We had ball games, camping and swimming trips, pizza parties, scavenger hunts, plays and skits, just to name some of the youth activities. Sometimes when there were problems, the girls confided in us.

Lucy's father was very strict and they were all in need of some counseling. They were, at first, very shy and self-conscious. I felt the father's intolerance was the root of some of their problems. For one thing, he would not allow the girls to wear jeans in public. Several times when we had outings or picnics at the Farm or Morris Park, the girls would wear a dress when they left home. They would don their jeans at a friend's house. This was in the mid to late 1950's!

Lucy finished high school and planned to enter the Mission field. She was reluctant at first to admit that her spiritual growth would lead to her chosen path in life (probably because of her father). We saw more love and concern for others develop in Lucy than we had seen in many adults.

Camp time came in August. Mary Flynn, a missionary from Africa and a Fairmont native, was one of our guest speakers. Mary inspired Lucy and one night they spoke until four o'clock in the morning. Lucy was ready to commit to the field of Mission. We contributed toward Lucy's tuition for formal training. Several staff members, Lucy's mother and I attended her graduation. After graduation Lucy was offered a job doing children's work at a Mission in Washington State. She liked teaching the children, but was not totally happy with some aspects of her position. Lucy later secured a satisfying position elsewhere. She regularly sends a gift of money to the Mission in Fairmont, remembering, no doubt, how much she was helped. Our family loved her so much. I thought as years went by what a tribute Lucy was to Miss Hampton and the experiences she had here at the Mission.

Footnote 1996: Lucy recently retired from a good position in Washington State where she was employed for thirty years. She now teaches bilingual students English. Lucy does volunteer work with youth who search for spiritual guidance.

Fred Holt "The Umbrella Man"

Fred was one of the most well known of all the people who came to the Mission. He owned a home at the edge of town. His father was a carpenter and had built the house many years before. Fred walked and walked all day, always with his umbrella.

After his parents' death, Fred lived alone in the house, mostly using just one room. A teacher heard that Fred was going to lose the home in payment of his parents' funeral bill. Joe went out to visit Fred to see what could be done. The house was in bad shape. It needed to be painted and fixed up and the plumbing needed repairs. The walls of the room you first entered from the front porch were completely covered with writing. On closer observation Joe saw what Fred had written on the walls; grocery lists and notes to himself of things he wanted to remember. No losing of a slip of paper for Fred! Fred received a small welfare check amounting to around forty dollars a month and that is all he had to exist on! Joe suggested the main house be fixed up and rented. Fred agreed to move into a smaller building on the property that had probably been used as a smokehouse. Joe went to the courthouse and made the proper arrangements.

Joe cashed in a few of his own war bonds and paid off Fred's debts. The Mission did not have any money to spare and the bonds were all Joe had besides his checking account. The idea was, the money collected for rent would go into a fund until the total amount of the loan was repaid to Joe. The house was rented to a family and the man agreed to do the necessary repairs for a smaller rental fee. I think they paid twenty-two fifty a month and lived there about two years. When another family rented the house we were able to rent it for thirty-five dollars monthly. After the loan was paid back to Joe, the rest of the money went to Fred.

The police called Joe one day saying they had been having a problem with Fred. Some boys had been teasing him for quite some time and he threatened to get after them with a gun! The police didn't want to put Fred in jail and wondered if he could live at the Mission. They asked if we could try to keep him from walking in that direction on his daily walks. We wondered how Fred would fit in at the Mission when he had been used to living alone for so many years. We did not need to worry. Fred was so happy to have three good meals a day, a new umbrella when he needed it or a pair of shoes. He wore out a lot of shoes! Fred didn't ask for much in his new home.

One day Joe observed Fred taking a dirty handkerchief from his pocket and using it on the door knob as he opened the door. Joe had a hunch why Fred did that, but asked anyway. Fred told him there were germs on that door knob! Joe said, "Well, I think there would be more germs on that handkerchief." Fred replied, "Yes, but they are *my* germs!"

I have always loved art, so I thought Fred would be an interesting subject to paint. After getting Fred's permission, I had a friend take pictures so I could paint Fred's portrait from one. I also had him come up to sit for me to get the right colors in his old army coat. I also wanted to make the portrait as realistic as possible. I was pleased with the results and entered the picture in a local art exhibit in the community. A hostess for the exhibit told Joe the picture of Fred was the most popular of all! She said people would walk up to the picture and would give a little gasp and say, "Well, that's Fred Holt." One evening several workers from the county jail came to see the picture. They told the hostess they wanted to see Fred Holt's picture. She led them to it. They looked, made comments and turned to go. She asked if they wanted to see the rest of the exhibit. They said, "No, we just came to see Fred!"

Fred was very ill once and Joe spoke with him about making a will. Knowing there were no heirs, they agreed it would be wise to will his property to the Mission. Several years after Fred died the sale of his property helped build Friendly Homes, a home for the elderly and disabled.

Fred became more feeble and his walks became shorter. One evening a man called and wanted to talk to Joe. He

Photo by George Batten

Fred Holt - "The "Umbrella Man"
    Fay Perry's portrait of Fred was the most popular ... some came just to see the picture of Fred!

wasn't in and so the man proceeded to tell me just what he thought of Joe's allowing Fred to be out walking! The man said Fred was walking along the highway when he saw him, and he could have been killed. I explained we realized that was dangerous but the only way to keep him in was to lock him in his room! We certainly would not do that. Fred was happy walking and would be very unhappy otherwise. We had to go get him when he couldn't make it home a few times. He soon became ill, was placed in the hospital and passed away a few days later.

Footnote: A fascinating newspaper article about Fred won an award for local writer Neil Shreve. "On Main Street" will be included in another compilation of Mission stories. In 1999 I donated the picture of Fred to a local museum. Betty Gill and other members of the organization were delighted to receive the portrait of Fred. The portrait was given a place of honor in the West Virginia Historical Society, next to the Marion County Courthouse. Other historical memorabilia found in Fred's home was included in the display.

Loretta Loudin

During the 1950's we came in contact with the Loudin family. Loretta and her many sisters and brothers faithfully attended all our activities. For years they attended our summer camps, services, youth rallies and sporting events. Jeannie, Loretta's younger sister, was the same age as Frani. They became good friends and Frani always called Jeannie's big sister Aunt Loretta. Sometimes on Sunday they would get together at our house or the Loudin's. Loretta was very interested in the Mission and helped in all our summer programs. She was a hard worker and had a great sense of humor. Spiritually motivated, Loretta was an excellent camp counselor.

After graduation from high school, Loretta was employed by a local glass factory. After being laid off in 1963, she gladly accepted the opportunity to work with Miss Hampton in the youth program. Loretta had many good qualities. Her strong voice was very effective in getting the children's attention and disciplining them. Because of her strong voice Joe gave her the nickname, Sarge! He loved to joke with her. All the kids loved "Sarge" and enjoyed her as friend and guide to look up to. She never married, but helped raise several of her nieces and nephews as the years went by. For many years Loretta was an excellent receptionist and secretary in the office.

When Friendly Homes was opened, Loretta became housekeeper on one floor of the three story building. Completing this activity in the morning, she continued to assist "Hampy" in the afternoon and evening. She was adept and happy to fill in wherever she was needed. Later, Loretta was promoted to manage the Helping Hand Store. Many times we were called on to help families who had lost everything in a fire. Large donations from the community of clothing, furniture, and other useful items were often more than we could give away to the families. We sold the unused items at the Helping Hand Store. People could browse and pay a small price for things they really needed or wanted. Some were happy to pay something, rather than accept charity. Another of Joe's quotes regarding what the Mission stood for was "Not charity, but a chance."

The store had grown over the years since the community donated so much. After we moved into the big yellow house, there were always boxes of clothing on our front porch! For a long time the "store" was right next to our house. The store also was one of the favorite projects of the Women's Auxiliary. They enjoyed sorting and pricing items for merchandise. This enabled them to play a big part in supporting the youth work. The Helping Hand Store became very popular in Fairmont. Always helpful and industrious, Loretta continued as manager when we moved to bigger and better locations.

Sometimes in the winter, charitable organizations had clothing drives to collect warm coats for the needy. A portion of the coats were donated to our store for distribution. Loretta and others helped many people find a warm winter coat. She told me of a boy who came in fairly late in the distribution process. Since she couldn't find him a coat, she remembered some other donated boxes of clothing. Looking in one box, Loretta found a perfect fit.

The jacket was even a popular design at the time. The boy was thrilled! Not too long after this, the boy's mother came in to tell us how her son watched TV all evening with his new coat on and refused to take it off! When he wanted to wear it to bed, she said she drew the line. We really laughed about this. Loretta is one of the most fun-loving, willing and faithful workers we ever had.

Footnote: When I retired in 1992, Loretta had been employed by the Mission for twenty-nine years. 2001 marks her thirty-seventh year of service and dedication.

Joe (in bow tie) was often guest speaker at meetings and banquets speaking of "Not Charity but a Chance."
"If Joe Perry were in business for himself he would be a millionaire!"

The Richards Family

The Richards family had nine children, seven of them girls. All of the girls attended our many activities, including summer camp. Jerry, the youngest boy, enjoyed being part of the Mission family. The oldest boy was the only one we did not have much contact with. Henry, the father, was a coal miner and in the early days did not have very steady work. He was a farmer at heart and most of the time they lived on a farm, at first renting one, later owning a farm. At times he held down two jobs to make ends meet. There were often long layoffs in the mines, but Ruth, his wife, managed well (when there was anything *to* manage). They were a close family. Much love was shown toward one another. The parents were fairly strict disciplinarians and seemed to be very wise with their children, as if by instinct. The first I remembered was Susan.

She came to camp when she was fourteen and her job was to sweep the dining room each day. As I was the camp cook, naturally I noticed her. Besides her play clothes, Susan only had two dresses to wear and one of them was torn. Joe called it to my attention one day and said, "Fay, do you think you could find a dress for that girl?" I replied that I didn't know, as she was such a tall girl. Most of the girls were close to six feet tall when they were grown. She wanted to attend college to become a teacher and needed a place to stay in town near the college. We were happy to help her move into the Mission.

Susan helped us during the camps we held during the summer. She attended two years of college then had to put school on hold for a year. Finances made it necessary that she get a full time job in a larger city. She stayed with some of her sisters who were living there. When she was able to come back to finish school, we did not ask her to work for room and board. We only asked her to help with special dinners or if we really needed someone to pitch in. Susan earned her degree and taught in a city south of Fairmont. She met a nice man there who taught in the same school. Susan and her husband have two children and live in another state.

A couple of years later Leah, the oldest girl, came to the Mission to live so she could graduate from the high school she was currently attending. Her family had moved to an area a distance away, making transportation a difficulty. She finished high school and I made her dress for graduation. Leah married soon after graduation and moved to a big city nearby. During Susan and Leah's stay at the Mission we were in contact with most of the sisters. They liked to visit them in their new home and attend our activities.

May, the fourth girl in age, loved to attend our activities, especially Miss Hampton's youth rallies, ball games, and clubs. May told us about a time when she was a little girl. The *only* present she received that year was the doll Miss Hampton brought her. "Hampy" also had dolls for all of May's sisters and presents for the rest of the family. May told me later that one Christmas morning when Miss Hampton arrived, she saw her mother at the stove, stirring oatmeal and crying. She couldn't understand why her mother was crying when they were all so happy! She was too young to know that her mother was happy, shedding tears of joy. May's mother was deeply touched that someone cared so much.

Leah, May, Loretta and I went to New York once to visit Miss Hampton's parents. On the way back, Leah related an incident that happened one school year when they were children. She said they were supposed to tell what they had for breakfast as a health lesson. When it came Leah's turn she said, "coffee soup" and fried bread!

She then explained, to her sister's further embarrassment, that "coffee soup" was weak coffee, sugar, and crumbled up day old bread mixed together!" In those days one teacher taught several grades, so sister Susan was present. Susan was shocked and embarrassed that her sister had "spilled the beans," so to speak. She later admonished Leah for telling what they really ate when there was nothing else.

One of the Richards girls married a young miner who

was killed about twenty years later in a mining accident. They had several children. She is thankful for the good years they had together. The youngest boy had a difficult time with the death of his father. He finally adjusted to his father's passing.

As of this writing Henry, the father, received "Black Lung" benefits and is doing well financially. He was able to purchase his first *new* truck. He and his wife are not well, but stay busy with all their grandchildren, as some live nearby. Henry spends his time doing beautiful leather work. Leah also lost her husband. He had many health problems. She is a proud grandmother and lives near her parents. We loved this family and were so happy we were able to see the fruits of our labor in their lives.

Ken

Ken was the son of "Grandma and Grandpa Harris," local radio entertainers of the thirties and forties. His wife Sylvia was in one of "Cowboy Cal's" popular radio trios.

Grandpa Harris came to the office to see Joe about his son Ken who was having a problem with alcohol. "Grandpa" hoped Joe could help Ken. The elderly father was very concerned about his family and Joe promised to try to see what he could do.

Shortly thereafter, Joe and I went to see Ken and his family. They had three precious little girls. Two were identical twins. We liked Ken and his wife Sylvia as soon as we met them and thought they had a wonderful little family. We counseled with them and invited them to come to the Mission for further visits or services. They soon were like family to us.

We knew when Ken was ready to get help with his drinking problem, he would. Ken was a salesman, traveling a great deal of the time and temptation was always there. Ken was a friendly person who liked being with people. He had an up and down experience with alcohol and some of the problems it caused. Joe often counseled with Ken and they became great friends. There were long periods of sobriety and we had hope.

Sylvia never gave up on Ken, although she must have felt like it at times. When things were too bad, Sylvia would give us a call. We always responded and tried to encourage her. One thing I'll always remember her saying was, "Joe, Ken is a good father and husband. Drinking and the things he does when he drinks, are the only faults he has. I know he loves me and the girls." She stood by him and they later moved to a southern state.

No doubt this move was the best thing that could have happened. Ken was away from old friends and had a chance to start a new life. He found a position which did not require traveling and he really settled down. Ken finally found a spiritual peace and is now enjoying retirement. On a Christmas card Sylvia wrote of Ken, "He speaks of Joe often, for he loved him very much. He often says how much Joe helped him to get his life started in the right direction."

I would love to visit them again and hear all the news concerning the girls and all the grandchildren.

Bunny

Bunny was small and wiry. She developed a deformity at the age of twelve. Bunny had a crooked back with a large hump on her left shoulder. She weighed around ninety pounds when she came to the Mission to work. Bunny's sister, Mabel, answered a newspaper ad we placed for a cook (I think this was in 1956). Joe hired Mabel and she asked if we could find work for her younger sister. Mabel had been working in a local restaurant. The owners also hired Bunny to bake pies. They requested that she only come in through the back door, fearing her physical appearance might upset the customers.

Bunny came to work at the Mission and never had to use the back door! She made the coffee and tea in a small kitchen adjoining the dining room. Through the years Bunny did many things. She helped with ordering supplies, groceries and gave out medications at mealtime. Bunny was a hard worker and never complained of being tired (if she was sick she tried to cover it up). She worked seven days a week, seldom missing a day. Employed at the Mission for thirty six years, Bunny died shortly after she retired.

I always said, "I'll have to retire if anything happens to Bunny." She became my right arm, reminding me of upcoming events, appointments, etc. I never knew anyone in Bunny's condition to live as long as she did. When she was sixty-seven, we had to take her to a nursing home. She passed away within a few weeks. I always thought the reason Bunny lived that long was because she was so active. Her heart and lungs were in good shape despite their crowded condition.

No one could have been more loyal than Bunny or Mabel. They both started calling me "mom" after their mother died. They were like family members. Mabel suffered a great loss with the death of her son, Petie Joe. She later was afflicted with Parkinson's Disease and died after having pneumonia in 1976. Bunny and Mabel lived in two other buildings in the Mission complex and later shared a nice apartment in Friendly Homes. Bunny loved children and was proud of our daughters and grandchildren. Janet and Frani were always anxious to see Bunny when they came for visits. Our grandson, Ryan Joseph Shoemaker, remarked recently, "When I think of the downtown Mission, I think of Bunny. I remember her most."

Footnote: We also loved Bunny's sister Jackie. She and her family lived in Fairmont and visited regularly. They contributed to the Mission from time to time and seemed part of our family. Frani loved to go with Bunny, Jackie and her children when they visited relatives in their home town.

Charley..."While there is life there is hope."

Charley came to the Mission because he was an alcoholic and had trouble holding a job. He came from one of the leading families in Fairmont. His cousin is an outstanding lawyer. Charley graduated at the head of his class from Alderson-Broaddus College. He was a newspaper man who worked at various jobs and was the editor of at least two that I knew of. Charley had a wonderful, rich bass voice and enjoyed singing solos at our services. One song Joe especially liked to hear him sing was "The Love of God." I never hear this song that I don't think of Charley. Charley would stay sober at the Mission until he found work elsewhere, or until he had the urge to drink. He was at Clarion, Pennsylvania, for a time and later was editor of a paper in Spencer, West Virginia. He would come back to the Mission when he failed -- when his drinking caught up with him.

One time, I remember feeling pretty disgusted with Charley. He was working at the Mission as our dishwasher. I happened to be in the dining room about six o'clock in the morning and saw him slip in the side door. He had been out all night drinking. I went to the house later and talked to Joe while he was shaving. I said, "Joe, I wouldn't put up with Charley any more if I were you. He does these things over and over again."

I'll never forget what Joe said in reply, "Fay, some day you *may* see Charley in Heaven!" He reminded me that "While there is life there's hope..." I am glad Joe never gave up on Charley. The last place Charley went to work was in Virginia, and we heard from him occasionally. He was doing well and singing in the choir of a church he attended. We were happy he was using his musical gift and staying sober.

One day the phone rang while I was in the kitchen. Joe was out somewhere and Charley's cousin was calling to tell Joe that Charley was in the hospital. Along with his drinking problem he had developed the habit of smoking. He developed lung cancer and was not expected to live. I was sorry to hear this news, but how glad I was that we had continued to help Charley through the years. It wasn't long until we learned that Charley had passed away. Joe attended the funeral with the cousin and his family. Later they turned over Charley's insurance to the Mission and the money was used to put in an intercommunication system, dedicating it to Charley.

Joe Perry - later 1950's "He reminded me that "While there is life there is hope'.

Charmaine

In 1958, a Fairmont boy met an attractive Thai girl in Southeast Asia. They were soon married in Asia and their first child was born with cerebral palsy. Much of Buddy's time was spent in a wheelchair, although he could walk very slowly with leg braces and the use of crutches. A second son, Larry, was born a year later. Shortly after Larry was born, the father returned to the states while Charmaine remained in her homeland, feeling at first reluctant to leave her people. After a number of months she changed her mind and applied for passage provided by the U. S. Government. Charmaine was flown from "Free China" to San Francisco, then to Fairmont.

Charmaine had decided to surprise her husband and didn't tell him she was coming to the U. S. The little wife from Taiwan was the one to be much more surprised. Her husband had fallen in love with another girl and married again! What excitement and embarrassment when the first wife appeared.

For a brief time Charmaine stayed with her husband's father, but she was very unhappy. We believe the father-in-law was very cruel to her. One day she left there and walked twelve miles into Fairmont seeking help. The authorities contacted the Mission, and we sought to make Charmaine, Buddy and Larry comfortable at the Mission. Her husband was held on a bigamy charge in the Marion County jail. If he were found guilty, it would probably mean one to ten years in prison.

Charmaine lived for three months at the Mission. This was during the Christmas holidays. She was liked by everyone. For Christmas she gave all her new-found friends a Christmas card with a dime scotch-taped to it. Charmaine faithfully visited her husband in the nearby jail and did his laundry each week. He made some faithful promises to her.

He was finally released in January and for seven months provided for his family. Around the last of July he suddenly disappeared and we had to step in to make provisions

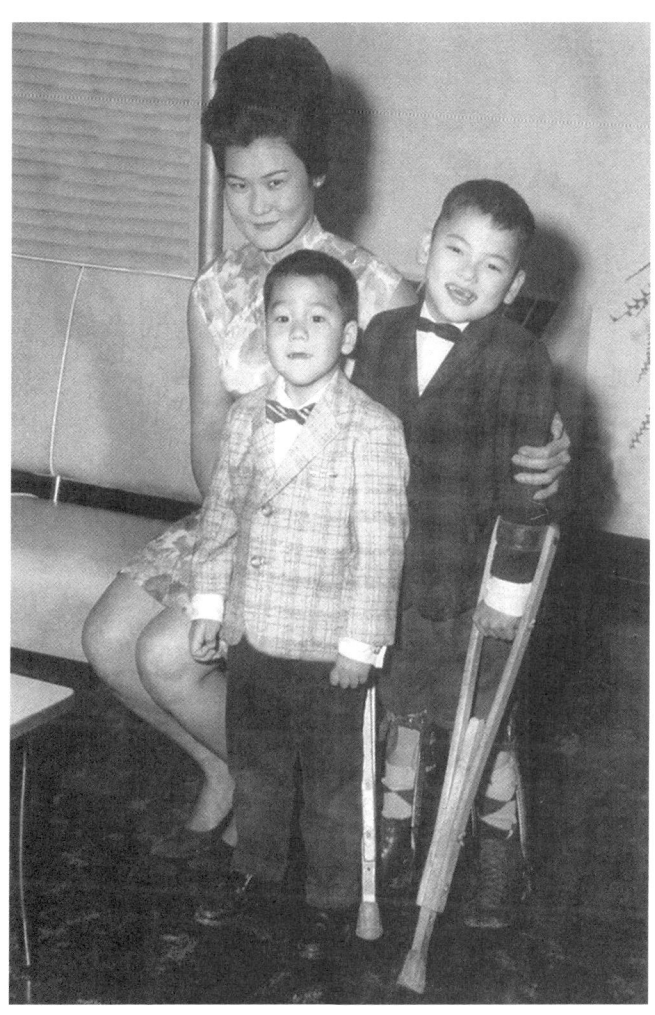

Charmaine, Larry, and Buddy

for Charmaine again until something definite could be worked out. At times she felt she would like to go back to her country but was uncertain. She had a friend in Florida who was from her country, could speak her language and wanted Charmaine to come and stay with her. Charmaine decided to remain in the Fairmont area.

Footnote: Charmaine remarried in 1969 and moved to a small coal mining community nearby. She stayed happily married to her second husband, Gary Taylor, a good provider and had another son, Jimmy. Buddy has had many operations and gets around well. During one of Charmaine's visits to the Mission I asked if she would like to have the portrait I painted of her and her two little boys. She was delighted! From time to time Frances Hampton and Wilda, her co-worker, visited Charmaine in her home. She was very happy, had learned to sew and do many things. Soon she suffered a great deal with arthritis. I saw her at West Virginia University Hospital once in later years when I was there with a resident of Friendly Homes. Buddy, now a grown man, saw me first and was very excited and happy to see me.

In later years Wilda saw Charmaine. She looked good, but tearfully explained to Wilda she was only expected to live two months. She was very happy to see Wilda, as she had been instrumental in Charmaine's spiritual growth. A month later Wilda learned that Charmaine died of cancer. Wilda was glad she had been faithful in her own mission in life. I will never forget the smiling faces of that beautiful girl and her sweet boys.

September 2001 - In memory of Charmaine, her husband, family, and friends also published and dedicated this poem in her native language:

They say memories are golden,
Well, maybe that is true.
I never wanted memories,
I only wanted you.
A million times I needed you,
A million times I cried,
If love alone could have saved you,
You never would have died.
Our family chain is broken,
And nothing seems the same,
But as God calls us one by one,
The chain will link again.

Joe Duchie

Joe was a little man of Hungarian decent who came to us in need. He had no home and was in his seventies. He was a very dear man who never wanted to be a bother. One day he came into the kitchen asking for some salt and vinegar. I knew this was a common remedy for a sore throat. I asked, "What's wrong Joe, do you have a sore throat?" He replied, "No, Missus, no sore, no can eat." I asked another question or two and realized that he might have a growth in his throat, possibly cancer. He was taken to a doctor that afternoon and it was determined that Joe probably had cancer of the esophagus and stomach. He was sent to a hospital in Phillipi, West Virginia, where he was given cobalt treatments. Surgeons also made an opening into his stomach through the abdomen wall and a tube was inserted to feed him.

After giving him the cobalt treatments for a few weeks, he was released, but they wanted a catheter inserted into his stomach each day to keep the place open. The measure was taken in case he needed to be fed through it at a later time. Joe Perry told the doctors we did not have a nurse, but he was sure I could do it! They wanted me to come to the hospital and let them show me just what had to be done. It was really very simple to do and for a year and a half I did not miss many days sterilizing the catheter, and inserting it into his stomach. This kept the feeding place open. They said a day missed now and then wouldn't matter. He was so appreciative and stayed fairly well. I only had to feed Joe Duchie a few times through the catheter.

As age and time went on, Joe was placed in a local hospital where he passed on a week or so later. His sister in Michigan was so thankful he had been cared for so well. She wrote two very nice letters. She was not well and couldn't come to the funeral.

George Stake

George was from one of the countries bordering Russia. He came to the United States to work in the mines as a young man. He was older now, rather bent and had a knee that slanted inward. George loved to work and we always tried to find something to keep him busy and out of mischief. He loved gardening and for a time we let him stay out at the Farm. He loved raising things, and the bigger the better, according to George. He would bring huge cucumbers in from the Farm and proudly show them off. He couldn't understand when I tried to tell him I didn't want cucumbers to grow that big, because they were not as tasty.

Sometimes George's imagination ran away with him. He thought someone was stealing his tomatoes and one day he went out to the Farm and picked bushels of green tomatoes! He wanted to pick them before they were all stolen. We were not very happy about all those green tomatoes we had to fry.

George was ill a few times. He always thought he was going to die when he was sick. One evening when I went into the men's dorm to see how he was doing, I decided he might have pneumonia and should go to the hospital. He agreed to go, but handed me something wrapped up in a brown, not too clean-looking handkerchief. It was one of those old snap pocketbooks for men and he had a few bills and some change in it. George said, "Here Missus, you keep. You and Mr. Perry, you same like Papa and Moma to me." He was in his late eighties then and I was in my forties! George was back from the hospital in a little more than a week and I gladly gave him back his money.

George liked to pick flowers and bring them to me, sometimes even dandelions or roses from a bush. I would have rather he left them on the bushes as the stems were so short it was not easy to arrange them in a vase. As it gave him so much pleasure to bring the flowers, I did my best to show proper gratitude for his thoughtfulness.

George was also a scavenger and was always picking up

things. Sometimes it was articles he had no business bothering with. We missed some tablecloths that we had sent to the laundry. They must have been mixed in with the sheets. George took the table cloths and put them between the mattresses on his bed. We discovered them a long time after we had missed them. Another time he took some pillow cases that Miss Hampton had been embroidering during handiwork time in her mothers club meetings. She missed them from her leather bag which she carried from meeting to meeting. When she asked George if he had see them, he pretended he didn't know what she was talking about. After George died the pillow cases were found in his old trunk!

Another time our truck driver, Mac, was instructed to bring a mattress from the farm to the Mission. The mattress was to be rebuilt by a factory for a day bed, so Mac put it on our front porch until morning. When I looked for the mattress it was not there. After inquiring about it, Mac said the mattress had been put on the porch. He went to the dorm and there he found that mattress on George's bed!

Mr. Peels

When Mr. Peels, an elderly man, first came to the Mission, his girlfriend came around quite frequently. Mr. Peel's girlfriend was always after money as she had a drinking problem. In a short while she died. Not too long after this, Mr. Peels started talking to me as if I were his girlfriend. One day he wanted to know when we were going to get married! When I explained that I was already married Mr. Peels became very upset and said, "Well, why didn't you *tell* me?" After that I played along with him, letting him think I was his girlfriend since I had a hard time convincing him otherwise!

Whenever Mr. Peels saw me across the dining room he would throw up his hand and call out quite loudly, "Hello, sweetheart." This always drew a big laugh from all the men sitting around the tables, and highly amused Joe and our kids. One day Mr. Peels approached Joe and asked him if he would perform the ceremony in marrying us. Joe told him he would and did nothing to discourage him. Joe got a kick out of the situation!

Dailey: Even a "Possum Rescued"

One man Joe encountered early in his dealings with the local Fairmont people was Dailey. A lovable and crippled black man, Dailey was an alcoholic and walked with a cane due to a very bad limp. When Joe first knew him, Dailey had a German Shepherd dog that went with him everywhere. He loved that dog. Some of the local police told Joe they used to have to arrest Dailey for drunkenness and the poor dog would hang around. They felt sorry for the dog and let him into the jail with his master. This was before we came to Fairmont. Often arrests were made for many local alcoholics who were housed in the city jail. The practice continued for a while after we came to Fairmont.

Dailey came to the Mission from time to time. During the 1950's and 1960's he made the Mission his home for most of those years. We all liked Dailey very much. He spoke often of the unending love of his wonderful mother. He loved to sing, especially "Leaning on the Everlasting Arms." I still think of him every time I hear that song, his favorite.

Joe, my daughters and I were given Fritzi, our first "Boxer," and Dailey asked permission to walk her. He felt so proud as he walked down the street with her on the leash. He said many times, "That dog has character!" In time, we were glad when a relative in California offered to send for Dailey. He was getting more physical problems and would need special care. He often had seizures and I think these resulted from some of the things he did in his early life. We missed him and wished him well.

Just recently Mac and I were talking about Dailey. He reminded me of a time when a local woman found an opossum in the laundry basket while in her basement. She called Joe! Mac, our truck driver, went after the "possum" and brought it into the dining room to show us. Dailey became really excited and wanted that possum in the worst way! He offered Mac twenty-five dollars for it. Knowing Joe would not want the animal killed and eaten, Mac refused. Instead, he transported the possum to the Farm and turned it loose.

Phillip Chubin

Phillip was a man who had lived in Barrackville, West Virginia, one the many coal mining towns surrounding Fairmont. There was no doubt he was a retired coal miner. He had become mentally incompetent and was sent to live at the Mission. He was very sweet and easy to get along with, but he deteriorated mentally as the years went by.

In those days there was nowhere to place a man like Phillip but in a mental hospital. If we had not been able to care for him, he would have lived in a mental ward for the rest of his life. Joe loved Phillip and did not want to see him go to Weston State Hospital. Sometimes Phillip would forget to put on all his clothes and wander around!

One morning I was walking our dog and the janitor was outside. He motioned for me to go back inside, and I wondered what was wrong and why he was waving me away. Then I saw Phillip behind him, clad only in his shirt! That wasn't too bad, but one night Joe was speaking to a large crowd in our auditorium. He glanced to the side door and there came Phillip with just his shoes on! He was calmly shuffling his way across to the other side of the room, right in front of the entire crowd. Joe calmly instructed a man to help Phillip out and down to the dorm. After that, Joe decided that we could no longer keep him. We had to let him go elsewhere with much regret.

Joe glanced to the side door and there Phillip with just his shoes on!   Joe Perry - 1960's

The Old Man and A Cup of Cold Water

I once received a letter from Dr. J. S. Maxwell, our first president of the Union Mission Board of Directors. The salutation was, "Dear Hostess of Angels Unawares." It took me back about twenty years or so.

Late one evening Joe met an old black man in front of our little chapel. When Joe asked what he could do for him he said, "I've come a long way today and if you could get me a cool glass of water I'd be very grateful." Joe came into the house and took a large glass, filled it with ice and water and took it to the old man. After the old man drank the water Joe told him he would take him down to the Men's Building and give him a place to sleep for the night. The old man said, "I am very tired, if I could just sit in here for a while I will be just fine. I can sleep on one of the benches."

Joe went over early the next morning but the old man was gone. We never saw him again. Joe remarked later about the odd feeling he had when he saw he was gone. He thought of the verse about "giving a cup of water in my name," and "entertaining angels unawares."

Melina

A social worker from West Virginia University Hospital called about a girl with mental problems in need of a place to stay. Joe was going to see someone in the hospital, so he took the opportunity to visit the psychiatric ward. Melina, a girl in her twenties, was sitting straight up in bed looking quite forlorn. When she saw Joe, she greeted him with a big smile.

We learned that Melina had a father but was living with her sister Ruth. The doctor thought Melina needed to be in another environment. The father made her feel inferior, saying she couldn't learn and putting her down in many ways. He was so critical and hard on Melina, her sister tried to make up for it by being too good. The sister didn't try to teach Melina to do anything around the house. I've never seen anyone with such low self-esteem. Melina's mother died when she was fourteen and that was another reason the sister tried to overcompensate.

We decided to let Melina come to the Mission to live. Her sister was to take her each weekend. I endeavored to teach Melina to wait on tables, prepare drinks and help with other small chores in the dining room. Melina was so insecure that every few minutes she asked, "How am I doing? Am I doing OK?" She would not only ask me but anyone else who happened to be near. At the same time I was teaching a new cook who had only cooked for her family, so it was a really nerve-wracking time. It took Melina about three months to be comfortable with her work. She finally learned to do a good job setting tables and accomplishing other tasks.

We learned that Melina had been sent to Charleston, West Virginia, for job training prior to living at the Mission. She had a learning disability. She could read and write reasonably well, was a good conversationalist but couldn't count money or tell time. A man, formerly head of Human Resources, attended a luncheon held at the Mission and Melina was helping to serve food. The man was so pleased to see her functioning so well. He had known her in Charleston and knew she "flunked out" there.

As time went on, it took all the patience I had, and a little more, to deal with Melina. She got on other residents' nerves so I let her come over to our house each evening to visit until bedtime. During the day she went to the "OP Shop" where she learned crafts and other simple skills. One Friday Melina's sister was due to pick her up. Melina said to me, "Mrs. Perry, did you ever see anyone like me?" I quite honestly answered, "No Melina, I *never* have." She laughed and said, "You will be glad for my sister to come so you can get some rest!"

We learned to love Melina and for three years she did amazingly well. One little step toward self-confidence led to another. It was heart warming to see her grow. Her sister was appreciative and certainly did her part to make Melina happy. One evening our cook told me of an incident. She told me that Melina was pouring milk for some of the residents. The cook said, "Melina poured one glass too full and what do you think she did?" Knowing the girl I replied, "She drank some of it!" We had to laugh even though it was not funny in one respect. The cook said, "I really told Melina never, never do a thing like that again! How would you like to have someone drink out of your glass?"

We had to watch Melina closely as she was only too human and liked fellows. At one point, before coming to us, she convinced her sister to let her get married! It had been a disaster and an annulment was granted. After a while Melina became increasingly rebellious and got the idea she might do better somewhere else. She thought she might meet a nice fellow and get married again! She began arguing with other workers, raising her voice and sometimes refusing to calm down. Melina just didn't care whether she pleased anyone or not. She would no longer cooperate, so I had to speak with her welfare worker who said, "Well Mrs. Perry, I can see Melina no different ten years from now. I think she has progressed as far as she can."

Joe was very ill at the time and I couldn't let Melina visit as often in the evenings. I didn't have time to give her the attention I had given in the past, so I made a very difficult decision. Melina would have to go elsewhere. I knew her sister would probably not find a suitable place and have to take Melina back into her own home. I felt sorry for Ruth, her husband and children. I felt badly for Melina. It was so difficult to give up on her, but I had no other choice. I kept in touch with Ruth. They never found another home for Melina, so she was living with them. My heart went out to them all.

Wilda Michael

A young girl from a very large family faithfully attended our many activities. She often helped Miss Hampton, our Youth Director, whom she admired very much. Her first contact with Frances Hampton was at the age of four. When it was time for Wilda to graduate from high school, she expressed a desire to follow in the footsteps of "Hampy," her beloved teacher and guide. Upon graduation she was able to follow that path by working in Pennsylvania and going to leadership training school part time. She stayed with some of her sisters living there.

After three years, Wilda went to Minnesota for a year to continue formal training in spiritual guidance for children who had many special needs. She was very interested in the Mission field, as she had practically grown up at the Mission. Miss Hampton had been an inspiration, someone to look up to. Wilda had so much respect for the way Frances had dedicated her life to service for others, especially underprivileged youth.

While in Minnesota, Wilda experienced a problem with her health and decided it was best to return home. Instead of being discouraged about not obtaining her teaching certificate, she knew there must be a better plan. Joe wrote her a letter and said, "come and see me when you get home and we'll have something for you." Wilda still treasures that letter. All the kids loved Joe so much and he loved every one of them.

She was soon invited to come to the Mission to live and work. She didn't have to finish college to further her education here! She already had hands-on Mission experience and fit right in with the staff. Wilda loved being of service to others, especially working with Miss Hampton. Her family had lived through some hard times so she really understood the physical as well as spiritual needs of the youth we were in contact with. Many were from really troubled or underprivileged homes. Wilda could see just how special these children were. There was a real connection between Frances and Wilda. It was known that Frances loved her like a

Friendly Homes opened its doors in 1969.
"Ashley makes the rounds with her, a tiny
Florence Nightengale."

daughter, and I know the feeling was mutual. Wilda continued working with Hampy (as we nicknamed her) until she died about nine years later. Hampy left a rich legacy for all her "Mission kids."

Wilda was asked to take over the position left vacant by Hampy. She agreed to try, even though she didn't feel capable of replacing Miss Hampton. She has done a good job using the outlines of her beloved teacher. Wilda has carved her own place in the hearts of the children and young people who come to the Mission. The children who came to the Mission always had so much fun! Wilda, with a hearty laugh and great sense of humor, still recalls Joe's stories and wit. In time, Wilda decided to adopt a child.

In the spring of 1984, Wilda adopted Ashley, a beautiful baby girl. The great granddaughter of someone we knew, Ashley was a year old at the time. The adoption came through on March twenty-ninth, the birth date Wilda's mother and I share! Ashley has a doting mother with lots of family members. Wilda was the first single parent in Marion County to adopt a child. Ashley is the also the child of parents who are of different races. Wilda knew she could find plenty of baby-sitters around the Mission! We were glad to have a little one around to liven things up and so was Wilda.

In October of that year Wilda changed jobs. She became our Women's Supervisor, taking over part of my duties of housekeeping, nursing and giving out medication at night. Ashley makes the rounds with her, a tiny "Florence Nightingale." One evening Ashley came to Friendly Homes and seeing her in the hall, I said, "Hello, Ashley." She came running with open arms and gave me a hug. I asked, "Where's Mommy?" She replied, "Goldie's room." Sure enough, that is where Wilda was. Ashley had learned all the ladies' names and loved visiting them. They were charmed by her and looked forward to her visits. Ashley looked so cute in her pajamas and carrying her doll. She was such a happy child, had a wonderful personality, and was very bright even at twenty months. I was happy to be Wilda's character witness before Judge Harper Meredith.

During this time Mr. Guggenheim, our current Executive Director, decided to find a man for the position of Youth Director. We had someone for a time, but eventually Wilda returned to her former position, directing the youth activities at the Mission.

Footnote: 2001 - Wilda Michael worked at the Mission until the year 2000, nearly thirty-one years. Besides the children's work and women's supervisor, she also helped in our jail visitations and office work. She is now doing personal home care in the Fairmont area. Of her many memories of Joe, she remembers most how he loved people. She still treasures the letter she received from Joe! Her daughter Ashley will graduate from high school May 26, 2001 and has been accepted to West Virginia University School of Law. Ashley, a tall, beautiful, yet sweet young woman is a real testimonial to "Hampy's kids," Wilda's determination, and to Joe's work. It was also a proud moment for me when I learned that Ashley, one of my 'adopted grandchildren', had been accepted to Law School and will begin in the fall of 2001.

Fay Learns to Drive

There came a time in later years when I really needed to learn to drive. Joe was not well and many times unable to drive. Those who could drive were very busy and I didn't want to bother them. At the age of fifty-six I realized I must learn to drive. It was the hardest thing I ever did!

At the AAA I was able to find someone to teach me, but I was his *first* student. He was an assistant coach at the college and this was a summer job. The worst part was he had been used to dealing with kids and young people, so he would lecture me when I made a mistake as if I were being careless. I was scared to death and certainly was not careless on purpose. He upset me and made me nervous. I was having a hard time finding someone to go out with me to practice and I think I only had about three or four practice sessions during the six weeks I was learning. Also, Joe was very ill and I was shouldering some of his responsibilities.

One morning was especially bad. I had to cook breakfast at the Mission since one of our cooks was not there. One of the men in Friendly Homes fell and I had to have the rescue squad take him to the hospital. All that was taking place and I was rushing to make my driving appointment on time. I did two dumb things and my instructor proceeded to lecture me on the importance of doing things right. I was so worked up about everything I cried a little.

Anyway, he did a good job of teaching me to park between those two barrels so I could pass my drivers test. I passed with flying colors and when I could take the station wagon out by myself, I really learned to drive. It was at least a year before I felt comfortable behind the wheel. I have been so thankful that I finally learned to drive. It has been such a help. I have been able to take people from the Mission to appointments, and, of course, take care of my own needs without bothering someone else. And if I do say so myself, I am a pretty good driver!

"Shotgun"

One Saturday afternoon, Jo Cottril, our Book Store clerk saw a boy standing on the corner of Washington and Jefferson Streets. The boy looked bewildered and lost. Jo called Joe and said she thought the boy needed some help. As it happened, our daughter Janet, her husband Dick, and Fran were visiting us from the D.C. area. Dick also observed, talked to the boy and realized he seemed in a daze.

We wondered if someone hadn't just dropped him off here, knowing he could get help. I prepared oven fried chicken for lunch at home that day. There was chicken and some other food left over. We were to have our annual spring banquet that night for the Mission's young people who had just graduated from high school. I left and went next door to the Mission kitchen to prepare food for the banquet.

Joe, in the meantime, learned that "Shotgun" had nowhere to go. Shotgun's stepfather had told him to leave. Joe could easily tell that Shotgun was having some mental problems and Joe's heart went out to this unwanted boy. Joe asked the boy if he was hungry and he shook his head yes. Joe took Shotgun into our dining room and asked Janet to find something for the boy to eat. She prepared a large plate of food with several pieces of chicken.

When I came back to the house later she said, "Mother, that boy was really hungry. I could have cried when I picked up his plate after he finished eating. Here, I want to show you. Look at these chicken bones! They look like they've been washed, they were licked so cleanly!"

Shotgun became a member of the Mission Family for sixteen years. When we first met Shotgun, he appeared much younger than his age. He was actually eighteen at the time he came to us. As I mentioned, Shotgun was like someone in a daze when he first arrived at the Mission. He wasn't able to do much except pick up one end of a bench or accomplish some very simple task. He was sent out to the Farm to work but he mostly stood around unless someone said, "Come here Shotgun, give me a hand." He was well liked by everyone.

With patience and time, Shotgun came out of his shell and learned to be a real help. Shotgun worked in our industrial department. He loved to ride "shotgun" in the cab of the truck when we picked up and baled scrap paper. I believe that is how he got that nickname!

At first, if you asked Shotgun a question he might answer you or he might not, usually not. He sometimes didn't know the answer or just didn't care to answer. It was summer and someone at the Mission cut his hair, almost shaving it off! I noticed there were a dozen or more scars on his head! Without thinking, I said, "Shotgun, what caused all those scars?" He didn't answer and I did not pursue the question as I had a hunch. After talking to Joe, I learned that Shotgun had been badly abused.

Shotgun was actually given two nicknames. For a while he was called "Herkimer" but the one that seemed to stick was "Shotgun." These names were certainly given to him with affection. He got along well with everyone and developed wit and confidence through the years. Fran always said Shotgun was like one of her "adopted brothers" who stayed at the Mission. Janet and Dick got a kick from hearing about his antics. Shotgun is now thirty-five (as of this writing, 1986). He has spent almost half of his life at the Mission.

Gerald

"Shotgun" was only at the Mission a month or so when a cousin the same age arrived at our doorstep under similar circumstances. This time, a welfare worker contacted us about the boy. He had some mental problems and was in need of a home. Gerald was more outgoing than Shotgun on first contact. He proved to be a good and faithful worker. He was another person who was loved by all.

Gerald was very neat and clean. He liked to dress up for church and was a fine looking young man. Shotgun, on the other hand, didn't worry much about keeping clean. He sometimes had to be told to take a bath and get clean clothes! Because Gerald appeared bright, I thought perhaps he could learn to read and write. A retired teacher was found to try to teach him. After a time, she gave up. He just couldn't learn, even though he wanted to very badly. He was here about three years when the Welfare Department decided to send him to a vocational school near Charleston, West Virginia. We thought it was a mistake since we felt Gerald needed our guidance and support. He was working here and earning more money than he actually spent. The only thing he was taught at the vocational school was to wash dishes.

It wasn't long until we had a letter from a girl who was less handicapped but had epilepsy. She wrote to us and signed the letter, "Your future daughter-in-law!" We were disturbed, but there was nothing we could do. Edna became pregnant and they were married. Gerald called, telling us that they had to leave her home; the parents were putting them out. They went to Charleston and Gerald found a job washing dishes at a restaurant. It wasn't long until they had two little boys and they called again. This time, the Welfare Department was taking the children. They didn't think Edna was able to care for them. Later, a brother of Gerald's moved in with them and the children were returned. Gerald and Edna came for two visits without the chldren. Edna called us "Mom and Dad," and we learned that was how Gerald referred to us. I am sure he secretly wished we were his parents. Edna and Gerald telephoned upon occasion.

They have had many ups and downs. Gerald developed ulcers and was never able to really earn enough to support a family. One time he lost his job because Edna hung around the restaurant too much, probably distracting Gerald. I was touched one Mother's Day to receive a huge card from Edna and Gerald. He was greatly upset to learn of Joe's death. I wonder many times how they are getting along, especially when I don't hear from them for many months or a year.

In February of 1986, Edna and Gerald came for a brief visit. They brought two of their children as the two older boys were in school. The only girl had a muscular problem. She was three years old, could barely sit alone and could not walk. She was a pretty child with curly blonde hair and large blue eyes like her father. I could hardly help but wonder how they coped with a handicapped child, but later learned they had some help. Their youngest boy was as cute as could be, bright and very active. He was named Joseph, for Joe Perry. He was about fifteen months old. The two older boys, close to their teens, were doing well in school. I wonder how Gerald and Edna will cope with teenagers. They enjoyed their visit, and they regretted leaving, especially Gerald. Besides visiting, Gerald needed to locate his birth certificate. I was fairly certain of his age. Since he was born in Marion County, his record was easily located. Just his mother's name was on the birth certificate with no father's name recorded. Through a relative of his I learned Gerald secretly "adopted" Joe and me as his father and mother. Gerald told me on his last visit that his step-father had beaten him with a corn cutter. I am not surprised the Welfare Department placed Gerald with us after that episode.

Gerald's mother seemingly did not care to keep in touch with him. I think I remember her seeing him once while he stayed with us. How sad she missed knowing a really sweet, loving son. Gerald has been a much better man than many I've seen who had more going for them.

Footnote 1996: A few years after writing about Gerald, I received a phone call from Gerald's half-sister. She said, "I hope you can help me find my brother, Gerald Morgan. He stayed at your Mission one time." I was happy to tell her that I was still in touch with Gerald, who now had a family. It seems that Gerald's stepfather died. The death of the stepfather allowed Gerald's sister and mother to get in touch. Gerald and Edna did not have a telephone, but I had their address in Charleston. I was able to tell the half sister that Gerald was doing well and the news about his family. She said, "You have made my day!"

In a few weeks I had a phone call from Edna and Gerald. They were in the Midwest with his sister and mother. His relatives wasted no time in going to Charleston to find Gerald. They took Gerald and his entire family back to the Midwest to live! I was so glad to hear this and to know the family would be there to help one another.

Still Later... I had a call from Edna and Gerald. They seemed very happy and they are now Grandma and Grandpa. He sees his sister about every day or talks with her on the phone. Gerald found his real family again, but he won't forget his adopted "Mission Family."

Stanley -- A Polish Emigrant -- Displaced Person

Joe went to Stanley's shack along the road to Farmington to pick up a man someone had called about. The man had been staying with Stanley but was sick and needed more care than Stanley could provide. As Joe was getting ready to leave Stanley said, "Someday when I get old, I'll come to your place to live."

"How old are you, Stanley?" Joe inquired.

"Eighty-seven," he replied!

Stanley did come to live at the Mission when he was eighty-nine. You cannot imagine the shack he had lived in. A friend called saying, "Joe, can you come and get Stanley?" Joe knew exactly who she meant and Stanley came to live at the Mission.

Stanley was given a room on the third floor of the Men's Building. He was quite content for many years. He liked to repair watches and his room looked like a disaster area, but he liked to be busy. Mary, one of our cooks, teased Stanley and told him when he was one hundred years old they would get married! One day he decided to put an electric bell outside the Mission's kitchen door so it could be rung at mealtime. (We had been using a hand bell.)*

Stanley built a small platform and climbed up to install the bell. Joe came along while he was working and said to be careful. To tease Joe, Stanley jumped up and down on the platform and did a little dance! He was ninety-three at the time.

When he was ninety-eight he received Black Lung Benefits and decided to move diagonally across from the Mission to the Fairmont Hotel. He lived at the Hotel until he had a stroke and was moved to a nursing home. He was one hundred three when he died!

Footnote: We loved Mary Lodge Harsh, our faithful, long time cook and her family as our own. *Frani loved to ring the hand bell, especially when she was small.

Stanley's shack was on the road to Farmington.

The "Kidnapper?"

The Hamptons, our Farm superintendent and his wife, had gone home to New York on vacation. Joe liked to go out to the Farm and stay as much as possible, partly because he loved being there. He also liked to have someone on the premises to prevent looting and such. One evening I answered the door and there stood a neatly dressed older man. He explained that he needed a place to stay for himself and his prospective bride. He told me the girl was underage and they had been to Maryland trying to be married, but they were not allowed to do so. They hoped to go on to Georgia as he thought they could get married there. I asked, "How old is the girl?"

He said, "She is over in the car, would you like to meet her?" I went with him, thinking this must be a tough young girl, one willing to marry an older man like this. I had the surprise of my life!

Here was a sweet, innocent, freckled-faced girl with long, straight, blond hair. She looked to be twelve or thirteen. Her name was Liddy. I sent the man to the Men's Building and talked with the girl. She told me that she had written to this man through a lonely heart's club! He told her that he was sixty years old. She had discovered he was seventy-two and was having second thoughts about him! He had visited her in her home but her parents had thrown him out. It seemed that her parents were most of the problem. She told me they drank and quarreled a lot, and she wanted to get away from home. She really didn't want to marry the man.

By morning the man had seen the girl in the Mission dining room and talked her into leaving with him. I spoke to Joe by phone and he advised me to call Charley Dodd, the Chief Deputy. I did so, but was informed that he was out on a stabbing case. I left my number and hoped he would call in time. He didn't call and the man and girl were getting ready to leave. To stall a little while, I asked if they would like for me to prepare some sandwiches to take along. He thought that might be a good idea. The couple were waiting in the car. I went to the dining room and told the cooks to prepare some sandwiches while I tried calling the Deputy again. This time I learned that Charley was on the way.

I took the sandwiches to the car and talked to them, trying to stall again, and was greatly relieved to see Charley walking between the buildings. He asked the man to get out and show identification, and then told him to come along to the office. They discovered that the man was wanted in Alabama for kidnapping. He was immediately placed in jail. The girl was sent to the local children's shelter for safekeeping until the authorities arrived from Alabama.

I later went to the shelter to see Liddy, but was not allowed to see her as she was kept in security. I was rather put-out about this but was glad when I received a letter from her about two weeks later. I corresponded with her for a time. I doubt if "the kidnapper" was in serious trouble, as I learned from a local dentist, the man was declared incompetent several years prior to this and had been committed to a veteran's home. I have often wondered what happened to the girl as she grew older. I certainly hoped she would find happiness in her life.

Footnote: Liddy thought the Mission was a wonderful place. She loved the older ladies who resided here. I am sure she would have been happy to hear me say, "Liddy, you can stay here if you like. Then you won't need to marry this man or go back home." I would have liked to say those words, but I knew I could not honestly do so, knowing she was underage and her parents had proper jurisdiction.

Sophie

A Department of Welfare worker from Grafton, West Virginia, called about a young woman in her early twenties. She was pregnant by a man nearly eighty with whom she lived. My first thought was "that dirty old man!" The worker told us Sophie was "slightly mentally retarded." Sophie came to the Mission and adjusted easily. She was well liked by everyone and gave us no problems whatsoever. Sophie was neat and clean and not afraid to work. I learned that she couldn't read or write and thought she could probably learn with help. I got in touch with a retired schoolteacher who attempted to teach her. The teacher said Sophie was slow but thought the young woman could learn to read in time.

After a short while I helped Sophie with her reading and tried to teach her when the teacher had to stop. Sophie learned quite a few words but had trouble retaining old ones after learning new words. I finally stopped trying to teach her as I knew she was just going to be here temporarily. All my efforts would be in vain since no one could take over after she went back to Grafton.

My feelings about the "old man" with whom she had lived changed after talking with Sophie week after week. Through the things Sophie told me, I realized that there was genuine love between them. The man was separated from his wife for years and Sophie, as a young girl, had gone to his home to do the cleaning. Later, when she was about fifteen, she went there to live. She was glad to leave home, as her home life left a lot to be desired.

There were several other children and the family was very poor. The home was crowded and dirty. Sophie had not attended much school. She had to stay home and help her mother, who was often sick. The old man taught her many things; how to cook, clean, and to tell time. They learned to love each other and when she learned she was pregnant, he planned to marry her. That is when he died.

There was no question in Sophie's mind that she would keep the baby. She had a beautiful baby girl and after a short while moved back to Grafton. Live-in arrangements were made with an older couple for Sophie and the baby. I heard from her for several years. Naturally, she had to have someone write the letters she sent to us.

One day when her daughter was about eighteen months old, Sophie brought her for a visit. She proudly showed her daughter off in a new dress and new shoes. There was no doubt in my mind that Sophie would be the best mother she could be under the circumstances. I have wondered many times how she fared through the years.

Footnote: Grafton, West Virginia, is the home of the very first Mother's Day celebration in this country.

Helen

I answered the phone one day when a lady inquired about coming to the Mission to live. I hesitated a little because there was a slight slur in her speech. Her voice reminded me of a woman named Ann, whose dad recently stayed with us for a while. Ann was addicted to barbiturates and there were problems when she went to various doctors for prescriptions. For this reason, I asked Helen to come in for an interview.

She arrived soon and I could see that she was a very nice person. Helen told me of her need of a place to stay for a while. After the death of her husband, she had been living with her sister in the area, but it hadn't worked out very well. Helen's sister thought she was overmedicating at times. When she contracted a cold, the cough medicine Helen took contained codeine.

The only place I could give Helen at the time was a room with two older ladies (Helen was barely fifty). She was glad to move in. Formerly an R.N., Helen had been working in a large hospital in Brooklyn, New York, for several years in the children's ward. She had developed emphysema and caught colds often from the children and was unable to work, sometimes for months at a time.

Helen applied for Social Security disability, but that hadn't come through and she had no income. The Department of Human Services helped with her housing until she was able to secure Social Security benefits (she had been a heavy cigarette smoker). In a few weeks we were able to put Helen in a private room. She was a delightful person to have around and her health improved to some extent. We had many talks and became good friends as time went on. I learned so much from her, as she was very knowledgeable in the medical field.

Later, when we needed an R.N. on the staff, Helen became our nurse. She kept the charts for the elderly people we had at the Mission. She monitored their medications and checked on them as needed. Since Helen could not go around people with colds or the flu, I took over that responsibility and reported to her. She was an excellent nurse and even performed artificial respiration for a patient who died.

I was able to take Helen to appointments and be with her when she needed hospitalization from time to time. In return, she was there for Joe and me when we needed her. I had surgery three times while she was with us. She came to see me nearly every day while I was in the hospital. One day when I found a lump in my breast, I went to Helen immediately. She didn't like the "feel" of it and advised me to see the doctor as soon as possible. I did so and in just a few days had a mastectomy because of the malignant tumor. It was in an early stage and I had a great recovery. No cancer cells were found in the lymph nodes and I chose not to have radiation or chemotherapy. There was no spread of the cancer.

Nine years later I developed uterine cancer and six years after that another mastectomy was necessary after discovering a small lump in my remaining breast. I am a three time cancer survivor, partly because of Helen.

As her emphysema worsened, Helen was on oxygen and had heart problems. Since most of her Social Security check went towards prescriptions, we didn't ask her to pay for room and board. She liked to help others with a little money when she could.

Helen complained of her side hurting from time to time. She thought it was probably gallstones. One night she called me about one o'clock in the morning and asked me to come to her room because she was very sick. I dressed and expected to take her to the hospital, which I did in a short while. After a day of testing the doctors thought she probably had a ruptured appendix and said she needed surgery. She asked to be transferred from Fairmont General to West Virginia University Hospital, where she had been receiving treatment. I accompanied her in the ambulance. Helen asked me to call her pastor. He and I stayed at the hospital while Helen was prepared for surgery.

After we saw that she would be all right, the pastor and I left at about five o'clock that morning. I had the thought when I got out of his car, "What would someone think if they saw me get out of his car at this time of the morning?"

Helen recovered in time, but had to be hospitalized when her heart weakened. I was with her in the I.C.U. all afternoon and evening. She said, "Don't you think you should take me *home* in the ambulance?" I reluctantly left the hospital that evening. This time she didn't come back. Helen had made prior arrangements to donate her body for medical research at West Virginia University Hospital. We held a memorial service for Helen in our chapel. We will always remember her and be grateful we had the opportunity to help and know this wonderful person.

Earl

Earl, an alcoholic, was one of Joe's favorite people. Earl loved animals and my husband shared that love with him. Earl was a "country boy" and had that homespun, whimsical way of telling stories of country life. He mostly worked on our Farm, staying in a small stone cottage and cooking for himself.

Joe's love for Earl was shared by our little four year old granddaughter, Cara. She stayed at the Farm one summer with my daughter Janet and her husband, Dick (they were both teachers and had their summers free). Our son-in-law wanted to help out because Joe was not well and needed more help at the Farm. Earl was good with children, talking to Cara, helping her pick up leaves and sharing experiences with her.

I remember one evening in late fall the Shoemakers, our son-in-law's parents, were visiting and we all went out to the Farm for a visit with the Hamptons. Cara wanted to go see Earl and Joe went with her. The time came for us to leave and Cara cried. She wanted to visit with Earl longer. When she climbed into the car she said tearfully, "Grandpa is lucky, he can visit Earl anytime he wants to!"

Earl was a good cook of plain food and he enjoyed having Joe eat with him from time to time. Joe knew it meant a lot to Earl for them to spend time together. Joe tried to spend as much time with him as possible to encourage him. It did help and Earl went long periods without drinking.

Joe was stricken with the "Lou Gherig's disease," A.L.S., and soon was unable to walk or stand alone without support. He still went to the Farm to visit with Earl. One Saturday morning Joe remarked that he felt terrible and didn't feel like going to the Farm that afternoon. I said, "Well, I wouldn't go if I were you." His answer was, "No, I am going to go. Saturday is a bad day and evening for an alcoholic. There is a bar not too far from the Farm. I promised Earl and I don't want to disappoint him." With the help of a man staying at the Mission, we loaded Joe and his wheelchair into the station wagon and I drove him to the Farm. Earl was there to help get him out of the car and into the cottage. I drove back for him late in the evening. I thought to myself, "How many people would put themselves out that much for someone like Earl?" I realized more than ever why Joe had been called to Rescue Mission work, and why he was so successful in dealing with those with special needs. They knew Joe really loved them.

Joe and Fay at Mission Farms, "County Miracle"

Gloria or Glenn?

The first time I saw Gloria she was sitting in the lobby waiting to see our Executive Director, Mr. Guggenheim. He was Joe's successor. She was dressed in a gray slacks suit and just looked different from the usual person who came to us for help, a little better dressed, for one thing.

A day or so later I saw Gloria painting the walls in one of the rooms in Friendly Homes. She was doing an excellent job and I got the impression she was trying to impress the others. She was working long hours, some nights until eleven. Gloria was paid very little for her work and I felt led to give her some money from my own pocket now and then. I knew she deserved it. It wasn't long until Gloria was doing other things and given the job of maintenance supervisor.

Gloria had a deep voice, walked like a man, sat like a man and seemed more masculine than feminine. Many expressed doubt that she was a woman. I remember being in Murphy's one day and Kay Heston, the saleslady, asked me that question, "Mrs. Perry, is Gloria a man or a woman?" Gloria cleared that matter up herself, by telling all, and I mean *all*. She actually had some surgeries involving the process of being female. Gloria gave her reason that she did it for God! It seemed that "she" was a man who had little to no control over sexual urges and thought it best to become a eunuch. Then she decided to become female instead. I felt I knew why. For one thing Gloria, formally Glenn, liked to attract attention. She usually went around in any old clothes, but one night she came to church in a suit, gray wig, false eyelashes and make-up! This gave away more than anything that she was really a man dressed as a woman. I thought Gloria had probably dressed like a woman going to bars as a transvestite, attracting attention and getting compliments. Liking the idea, she decided to have surgery to become a woman.

She also liked to excel and in a man's world didn't get the attention she craved. Gloria did excel. She did beautiful work in many ways. She could repair a TV, furnace, do electrical work, plumbing, carpentry and just about anything we asked.

Gloria even fixed Fran's car one time when it was a basket case. She had been driving from the D. C. area in a snowstorm. She was coming home for Christmas and had a Mercedes at the time. "Molly," as Fran named her car, just died on the road! We went to get Fran and had Molly towed to Fairmont. Gloria took the motor of the car all apart and put it back together again! Parts were scattered in the trunk, back seat, everywhere. No one else we knew could attempt to put it back together. Fran used the car for some time before she needed any more repairs.

On the other hand, Gloria had a problem getting along with people, especially anyone in authority. She was jealous of anyone well liked by others. There was usually at least one person she was giving a hard time. While she was here Gloria completely overhauled the furnace, putting in some electrical parts that no one knew how to operate after she left. She did some fine cabinet work in our dishwashing kitchen and remodeled a kitchen in the Carleton house. The house was willed to the Mission some time before. Gloria moved a door, put in a window and installed beautiful cabinets. It really looked like a professional job.

Everything was fine when Gloria was in a good mood. If she was angry with someone, or about something, she was hard to live with. She would go around for days ranting and complaining, with her face looking like a storm cloud. Gloria also didn't like to change clothes very often. She didn't see a reason to change clothes when she was going to be back doing dirty work again! All the times Gloria worked on the Carleton house she didn't change her clothes. It was about six weeks. At first, I very diplomatically suggested she change clothes. I even offered to have them washed for her. Finally, I told her that the odor was offensive. It made no difference. One time, I went to the office and I knew Gloria had been there because the odor still lingered!

One of her worst faults was trying to cause discord among staff members. Gloria was not very successful at this.

Toward the end of her stay, she did a fairly good job of brainwashing one lady who also stayed here. This person, a good friend, could see Gloria's faults as well as her good qualities but overlooked her anger once too often.

Even though Gloria did not care about her personal appearance, she had expensive taste in electronics. She loved to buy things. I loaned her money for her first stereo and she kept buying more expensive ones, better TVs, a movie camera and a computer, among many things. She worked part time for Hartley's department store, and when she left the Mission she owed them more than five thousand dollars.

Gloria threatened to leave many times, usually attempting to get her way about something. Toward the last, she wanted to turn some rooms on the Mission's top floor into an apartment! This meant she would spend a lot of time and money on a project we were not interested in doing. In a way, we were hoping Gloria would leave. When Gloria saw the tactic of threatening to leave was not working, she used her friend to plead her case so we would let her stay! She really wanted to stay in the worst way.

The main reason we really were glad to see her leave was that she became a hindrance in our work with the younger women who came for help. Some were promiscuous and Gloria called them "whores" and put them down at every opportunity. She became very angry when she was put in her place for saying those very words. I think Gloria stayed as long as she did because she was, more or less, in hiding. She had a car and only drove it a few times. When the battery went dead and I offered to buy her another, she didn't seem interested. When her operator's license expired she did not get another one. Gloria loved to drive. She told someone she had two DUI charges in other states and we were fairly sure the car was not paid for.

Gloria moved to California and for a time had difficulty finding work. She sold many belongings to have something to eat. She was living in a small apartment owned by a friend. It wasn't long until Gloria was asked to move out. She was able to get temporary employment and then obtained a good position with an electronics firm. She earned eighteen to twenty-five dollars an hour, quite a contrast to what we could pay.

I do know that Gloria was by far the most intelligent person who stayed with us. She must have had a very high I.Q. On the other hand, Gloria had very little common sense. In many ways, we felt sorry for her as she was often unhappy. I wish we could have reached her, but it was impossible. Gloria thought she had all the answers and the problem was *always* with others. She was never wrong in her opinion!

Besides her many talents, Gloria did have some other good qualities. She was very kind to those who were handicapped in any way. She also could be accommodating when she wanted to. Gloria would fix a TV on her own time or run errands for the shut-ins. These people missed her after she left the Mission.

Footnote: Early 1990's - Gloria calls from time to time and would love to come back here to work. She says she has friends here and in California she has no real friends. We know it would not work out. We could certainly use Gloria and her many talents, but, with all things considered, we know it would not be for the best.

1998: Gloria called recently still wanting to come home. She stated that she no longer "had boobs!" I think she, now HE, changed back to get his Navy pension. As far as I know Glenn is in a Navy retirement home. Once during "Gloria's" stay at the Mission she boasted that "she could con a hungry man out of his steak!"

The Domingues Family

In the latter part of July during the 1980's we were called about a family in need of a place to stay. This family was the largest and one of the nicest to occupy our Family Shelter. Actually there were two families, all traveling together in an old Greyhound bus. The bus had been renovated into living quarters for the families to travel in during the summer months.

Miguel Domingues, the father of one family, did construction work in the U. S. during the school year. He was originally from Cuba. When vacation time came, Miguel drove his family to Mexico in the old Greyhound bus. They distributed food and clothing they had collected in the U. S. Miguel gave these items to the people in the poorest parts of Mexico. The family then came back in the bus and ended the summer with a trip to New Jersey to visit his brother.

Maria Perez was a friend of the Domingues family. Maria's husband had been shot three months before we met them. Miguel promised Maria's dying husband he would help look after the Perez family.

This time, the Domingues were on their way back to Houston, Texas, where Miguel planned to work. They had about a thousand dollars for gas and food. Miguel was on Interstate 79 and saw the sign for "Houston, Pennsylvania." The bus broke down near Fairmont and was towed into a local garage. At the garage the family was told of the Mission and all eleven of them arrived shortly!

The family seemed to enjoy their stay at the Mission. Miguel's oldest son liked our food. He told the cook one time, "You all cook the best food! Could you give me the recipes?" Miguel soon learned that repairs would be more than two thousand dollars. The families had been with us nearly a month and were going to need some financial help to get on their way. It was almost time for school to start so I decided to call John Veasey, Editor of the *Times West Virginian* newspaper. After speaking with John, I took Miguel to the newspaper office to be interviewed. The next day after the story appeared in the paper, there was immediate response.

John Manchin called from Farmington and asked me to bring Mr. Domingues to see him. John wrote a check for five hundred dollars and handed it to Miguel. John later helped Miguel in other ways, besides calling a friend of his who was generous to the Domingues family. Soon, a man walked into the Mission and gave me a check for the family. Other donations started coming in. We had enough to pay the repair bill and the day the Domingues family was ready to depart, I'm sure some people in Fairmont wondered what was going on when they saw that bus sitting on Washington Street. The entire family, as well as many from the Mission family, were out to say good-bye and wish them blessings as they journeyed back to Texas. The children didn't want to leave and we didn't want them to go!

I heard from Miguel's wife at Christmas but have not heard since. Helping the Domingues family was truly a unique experience. I felt sure that Divine intervention had a hand in this family getting lost on the interstate. Where else could they have found the accommodations they found at the Mission? Fairmont's friendly people also played a big part in coming to the aid of the Domingues family.

Footnote: It was interesting to hear Miguel tell about Cuba. He escaped to Guantanamo Bay, swam across the bay and was picked up by our servicemen. He had been badly stung by jellyfish while crossing the bay. After a week he was sent to Miami. Later he went to New York. Still later in 1974 he met he met and married Rose, an American citizen. They became the parents of three children. Maria Perez was the mother of the other five children. Maria spoke very little English. She really needed and appreciated her "adopted" family.

The Domingues family - Miguel, upper left, his older son, right. Mrs. Domingues, left front, Mrs. Perez Miguel's oldest son told our cook, "You all cook the best food! Could you give me the recipes?"

Sandra and Mac

Looking back to the earlier days of the Mission I am reminded of two people who have remained a constant throughout these many years. The first time we saw Sandra, she was living in a house near the Mission with her mother and father. Sandra was eleven years of age, an attractive girl with dark hair and big brown eyes. We learned that her mother and father were both alcoholics. Many times my youngest, Frances Jean, would be outside on our large front porch in her playpen. Sandra would come along and talk to her.

Frances Hampton and Martha Nelson, our youth workers, decided to take Sandra to summer camp. Even though she was a little younger than the other children, Sandra fit in well with all our activities. Sandra had a beautiful voice and loved to sing. I remember how thrilled I was the first time I heard her sing, "Great is Thy Faithfulness." Sandra had just recovered from an illness commonly called St. Vitas Dance. This caused to her to be a very nervous child. She also had rheumatic fever which resulted in heart problems later in life.

When Sandra was thirteen her father died. He had been drinking heavily and died in a building near their house. He had been dead for several days. Joe conducted the funeral and our hearts went out to Sandra. Her mother was living with another man and Sandra was very unhappy with the situation. Sandra wanted to come to the Mission to live and it was all right with her mother. At that time, John and Betty Garber were here with their children, Dennis and Dale. John was Joe's Assistant Superintendent. The Garbers needed someone to help look after the children, so Sandra moved into their apartment in a spare room. The Garbers welcomed another son, David, while they worked here. Later Sandra moved into our Main Building, where we had living quarters for women. She was attending high school at the time.

Joe set up an account to bank the Social Security check she received each month. The money was saved for further schooling. Even though the check was only forty-seven dollars a month, by graduation there was almost enough money to further her education. During her last years in high school, she helped in the Mission dining room.

I remember once when I took Sandra to Hartley's department store to buy her a new pair of shoes. We had a good laugh when she removed one of her shoes and found a bobby pin in it. She said, "Those old shoes hurt so bad I didn't notice!"

Sandra decided she wanted to go into training to prepare for service in the field of Mission work in some way. The good works and love toward other people she had seen growing up at the Mission had a positive impact on this young girl. She indeed had a family, her "Mission" family, and was loved by all.

When she came home for Christmas vacation during her second year away at school, she met a young man, several years her senior. They met in the laundry room at the Mission. It was a mutual attraction, but at first we were very worried. Charles was a parolee and had only been living here a short while. A remark he made to another man added to our worries. After Sandra returned to school she corresponded with "Mac," as we called him. Evidently, Mac could tell she was getting serious about him. Mac said to one of our other men, "I'd better cue her in!" By that we thought he was not thinking too seriously about her. Before long we realized he did care for her deeply.

Charles, as I said before, was a parolee. He was sent to Moundsville Prison on a breaking and entering charge. He was in trouble before that and as the judge sentenced him he said, "I don't ever want to see you involved in robbery and in my court again!" George, a friend and brother-in-law of Mac's, was involved in the robbery and wounded in the arrest. After Mac served twenty-two months he was eligible for parole, so his mother came to see Joe. She wanted him to be her son's parolee advisor and give him a job. It was done, but Mac came to the Mission, at first, with a huge chip on his shoulder. He didn't like to attend our services or obey any of the rules he had to abide by.

After being here about four months he began to realize a spiritual power much greater than his own. We no longer worried about Mac and Sandra dating. "June" talked to him and prayed with him one night. June had a way of speaking to the hardest of hearts, even Mac's. After that night Mac was transformed by Divine grace.

We learned that Mac came from a poor family and his father was a drinking man who did not provide very well for his family. Mac told me one time he did not have a coat or sweater to wear to school, so an uncle bought him a sweater. Mac went on to say that if one of the boys in the family had a new pair of socks, he didn't *dare* remove his socks to wash them. If they did one of the other kids would steal them!

Mac had not attended school very faithfully and his grammar left something to be desired. Mac was extremely intelligent and learned to speak very well. Mac helped Sandra financially during her last year of school. After graduation he bought her a wedding dress. Frances Hampton paid for the flowers, cards and favors, and I saw to the wedding cake and refreshments. They were married in the Mission auditorium and we had the reception in the Mission dining room. The only thing that marred the wedding was that Sandra's mother didn't show up.

At the last minute they went out to try and find her. She was not to be found, as she was out drinking. There were several members of Sandra's family present as well as Mac's and some from the Mission family. Oscar was told he could come to the wedding, but had to get dressed-up and couldn't wear his old and tattered overalls. Oscar dressed-up, looked like a different Oscar, and came to the wedding. When Mac looked for him after the ceremony to take pictures, Oscar had already gone to the dorm, took off his good suit and had those overalls on again!

After a short honeymoon Mac and Sandra came back to the Mission and moved into a basement apartment in the former West property near the Mission. Mac expressed a desire to go into the ministry, so he completed a correspondence course to begin the process. In about a year they had their first and only daughter, Ellen. I felt like a grandmother and sometimes baby-sat with Ellen while her mother helped Miss Hampton.

During this time Mac was growing spiritually and emotionally. He was so very shy in the beginning and suffered from an inferiority complex. I was pleased with his sincerity and loved to see his broad smile. It was a proud moment for all when he attended ministerial school and received his diploma. Mac, a handsome young man, was probably the first "parolee to pastor" in Fairmont! During this time Rex and Randy were born. In 1984 they thought their family was complete. They soon welcomed another son, Ryan. It was like starting all over again. They now have three grown children, a grade-school child and a grandchild.

Footnote: Mac has served in several churches. Sandra, faithful in service to nursing homes, families and others, has created her own ministry. She is active in helping Mac with his duties. Mac and Sandra recently celebrated their 25th wedding anniversary. They are proud of their daughter, Ellen, a graduate of the school her father attended. Rex, their oldest son, was an outstanding Aviation Machinist Mate in the Navy. In 1984 he received a medal in recognition of "professional achievement in the superior performance of his duties." Rex was presented the citation by T. F. Brown, Rear Admiral U. S. Navy, who said, *"His enthusiasm, knowledge, and total dedication to duty reflected great credit upon himself and were in keeping with the highest traditions of the United States Naval Service."* Rex was a AAA all state football punter in high school. Mac and Sandra have been thankful for the Mission and Mac is often our camp speaker. When Joe passed on, I asked Mac to tell his own life story at the funeral. I am so glad I did, as when Mac was speaking we realized that Joe's work was not finished. Each young life we were fortunate to guide along the way would carry on the spirit of the Mission in their own chosen path. It was really an uplifting service.

These stories have revealed the highlights
of a rewarding lifetime of mission work.
Many are left untold of people now living
throughout the country, who were
helped and loved.

The history of the Union Mission
in Fairmont, West Virginia,
gives inspiration for today's
even more desperate need.

Joe & Fay Perry Story
Part Two

In 1951 doctors had given up hope for the survival of Fay Perry. Faith in prayer alone prevented her from dying when all seemed hopeless. She had been hemorrhaging for several days and finally remembered that she had not prayed specifically for the bleeding to stop. Doctors were amazed an hour or so later when they found no more hemorrhaging. After a long recovery period as a result of this extensive and experimental surgery for ulcerative colitis, Fay was able to resume her many responsibilities.

Joe also experienced illness and disease. He endured heart ailments and high blood pressure, most likely because of extreme stress. Also plagued with the sometimes debilitating and little known illness named chronic depression, he at times struggled inwardly. In the mid-1960's Joe fell from a ladder while climbing to the roof of a two story house. The ladder inadvertently was placed on icy asphalt (black ice). This took a major toll on Joe physically as well as emotionally. It was very frustrating for a man like Joe Perry to slow down with crutches and canes. In the late 1960's he had surgery for serious blockage of a main artery in the neck. Another main artery was completely blocked. It was later determined that arteriosclerosis had been developing for some time. Joe knew he had a fifty-fifty chance of survival. He did survive and continued to work unfailingly on behalf of those in need. He carried on his work and continued to perform amazing and extraordinary tasks for humanity.

In the early 1970's Joe was not well again. It was a dark day when Joe Perry was diagnosed with A.L.S., commonly known as Lou Gherig disease. As his condition worsened, people from far and wide called and sent letters. Because of his well known good works, articles, banquets and salutations were a way of life. Joe, never desiring fame or fortune, was one of the most well known and respected men in Marion County and surrounding areas. John Veasey of the *Times West Virginian* newspaper enjoyed writing about the feats of Joe and Fay Perry and the miracle Mission just down the street. After the announcement of Joe's illness, the headline of one article read; *"Honor is Long Overdue for Joe Perry."* Joe once received an award for Humanitarian of the Year. He was also once voted Fairmont's "Good Sam," and named Man of the Year at least once. For many years the Mission had come to represent a haven of mercy, a lighthouse to the lost and an unshakable landmark.

It was once noted when hospitalized, he laughed and remarked to Fay after looking around the room at the other women visiting their husbands, "Maw, you're a beautiful woman, and you don't have a bad shape either!"

Joe lived with A.L.S. for nearly two years, longer than most in those days. He remained sharp in wit, mentally alert, and was fortunate to find a successor, Bob Guggenheim. Joe still read and loved to be driven out to the Mission Farm. Only the last four days of his life were spent in the hospital. Watching the news and joking with his roommate, Joe Perry gracefully passed on at age sixty-six. His body was laid to rest at his beloved Mission Farm just beyond the community of Quiet Dell at Glady Creek. During her sixty-two years of service at the Mission, Fay sometimes dealt with arthritis or required additional surgeries. A three-time cancer survivor, she never required chemotherapy or radiation treatment.

In October of 1999 Fay was again very ill and not expected to live. In March of 2001, just before her eighty-fifth birthday, Fay experienced serious kidney disease and other physical problems. She miraculously bounced back again. During Fay's long life as the Mission's "mom," she has made an enormous impact in the lives of thousands of people.

Throughout its sixty-four year history, the Mission continues as a haven for the less fortunate in our presence, and a monument to the vision of Joe Perry. Fay Perry's unending devotion of twenty-four years after Joe's passing, serves as a tribute to her unconditional love and belief in his "dream of a place where a stranger could be taken in."

Still a heart for the children after 62 years in Mission work.
Spring 1999 - Fay Perry & Kesean Stuck
("Loretta Loudin" story - Loretta is his aunt.)

Fay needed more personal care and moved from the Mission for the first time in her life. She lived with her daughter and son-in-law, Janet and Dick Shoemaker, in Walkersville, Maryland, for nearly two years. As of this writing, she resides at a personal care home near her daughter. It is truly "Just One More Miracle" that she lived to see the completion of the book, More Done Than Said. The work of Joe and Fay Perry will be carried on through her very own words and stories of the Mission and its people.

The indomitable spirits of Joe and Fay Perry live on in the hearts of all whose lives they enriched. It has been said that behind every great man there is an incredible woman. Fay Perry was often the strength behind the man and the Mission she so dearly loved.

Fay Perry recently celebrated her eighty-sixth birthday, on March 30, 2002.

..."to rest at his beloved Mission Farm"..."'by the side of the road.'"

The Union Mission Corner

"The Old Rock House-Old Bones Place, a Fairmont Mystery"

(Editor's note: This edited feature article by Glenn Lough, county historian, tells part of the story of two historic landmarks within the boundary of Mission property.)

"In the late 1970's when the home of Joe and Fay Perry was razed, the mystery of the "Old Rock House" was brought to light.

Until recently a portion of Middletown Lot four on the corner of Washington and Jefferson Streets was occupied by the home of Mr. Joe Perry, most favorably known as superintendent of the Union Mission. Joe and his family lived there for many years. The house being razed is on the same location where, long ago stood the "old rock house." The large oblong dwelling and huge rocks buried eight feet deep were considered a mystery.

In 1750 the old rock house was found by early settlers. Parts of the wall were still standing. The floor was laid with finely ground mussel shells. Pottery, arrow points and spearheads made of flint and quartz were discovered. A flint axe blade was among other artifacts. A huge oak tree grew from inside the rock house. The tree was judged to be over three hundred years old. *It grew from inside the rock house long before* the Revolutionary War.

Surely, the old rock house was the first dwelling of any known nature that ever was inhabited within the bounds of our county. Near the house was found a large fire pit with signs of fires penetrating the earth for several feet below the surface of the earth. This is indeed a profound mystery.

In March 1822 the bones of four adults, one infant and a large dog-like animal were unearthed and considered to be those of American Indians. The bones, buried some three hundred years before, were reburied below the old rock house. Thus began the addition of the "old bones place" legend to old rock house folklore. This folklore, confirmed by numerous writers of history, is rich with vivid descriptions of this strange and ancient structure.

In the late 1880's many huge rocks unearthed from the old rock house, were used for the foundation of Marion County's very first court house. This historic building later became a church."

paraphrased and quoted....The Fairmont *Times West Virginian*

Left - bookstore, house, chapel (later store), Friendly Homes, Main Bldg. (behind) "Long ago stood the 'old rock house,' considered a profound mystery." (where house is)

With the addition of this property, the former court house/church (pictured on right, page 183) the Union Mission owned the entire city block of buildings. By no coincidence was the Mission located on this historic and hallowed ground.

The "most historically important landmark in downtown Fairmont." Huge rocks in foundation unearthed from the "Old Rock House."

This old church is the "most historically important landmark in downtown Fairmont." The fact that the first regular session of the Marion County Court (before 1844) was held within the walls of the original old brick church gives certain historical luster possessed by no other landmark. It is, indeed, a rare historical possession. The first services were held on New Year's Sunday, 1842 in "old Fairmont," formerly known as Middletown. The church, considered unsafe, was razed and rebuilt in 1880 on the original "rock house" foundation. This red brick building was the final acquisition to the Mission block.

APPENDIX

Footnote: "Dan's Story"
When Joe was bedfast with A.L.S., Dan called one night saying that all of his children were there. His wife played the piano and they all joined together to sing a hymn for Joe over the phone. Joe was pleased and told Dan he had made his day! It was just a few weeks after this we learned that Dan had a heart attack and died. We were surprised and saddened to hear of his passing, but were glad we had a part in helping Dan.

Footnote: "The DeLuca Family"
when my husband died after thirty-eight years in Mission work, I received a letter from Mrs. DeLuca's sister. She wrote, "If it had not been for you and your husband, my sister and her family would have starved." We were happy to help this most deserving family. This statement of Mrs. DeLuca's sister made me remember what someone else said when he visited us back in Fairmont. The man said, "I don't know what we would have done when we were kids, if it had not been for Joe Perry!"

Footnote: "The Hawkins Family"
Amos, the oldest boy, was about thirteen when we arrived in Fairmont. He was so much like his mother, with the same soft manner of speaking and very kind heart. After his father died and all the children were grown and gone, Emma moved in with Amos and his wife and they lovingly cared for her. I'm sure her happiest days were in those later years.

Footnote: Frances Hampton passed away in the 1980's. Her sister Elizabeth Hampton currently resides at a home for retired nurses near Cortland. N. Y.

"The Church on Wheels"*

This amazing work of art was built by Joe and the men during the early 1940's.

Little is actually known how "The Church on Wheels" came about. Joe was probably joking about somehow taking a church to those who couldn't get to the Mission, those who lived in distant coal mining communities or hollows, known as "hollers." One of the men most likely said; "Hey Joe, we could build one."

"Yes," Joe would have replied... "on wheels!"

And so they did. That is how it was. Whatever Joe said got done. He had a unique gift of bringing out the best in people. They knew how much he loved and cared about each one of them.

It seems unimaginable that Fay Perry doesn't remember much about this endeavor! She was obviously busy in the kitchen or elsewhere and not caught up in this particular brilliant idea, one of Joe Perry's many visions. When asked how the portable church came about she says, "I don't know any more about *that thing!*"

The known facts are "The Church on Wheels" was built during gasoline rationing. Stamps were used instead of money. The material used to cover the wooden frame was a type of siding made to look like brick, very popular on houses during that era. Joe and some of the men actually did the construction of this "work of art."

The "Church" was driven from behind the Mission property on Cleveland Avenue to Tenth Street. The infamous church never got beyond Tenth Street, not much more than ten blocks from the Mission, due to the gasoline rationing! A few services were held inside. A small pump organ was used for music and ten to twelve people could be seated at one "service." Imagine the curiosity and excitement when the people of Fairmont saw the portable church coming down the street!

*See photograph, page 61

Brief on J. T. S. "Flintlock" Perry - Joe Perry's grandfather. See photograph, page 101 The headline and recollection of a large newspaper article about "Flintlock" read:

"Dual Lynching Party in 1876 East of Charleston Recalled"

Negro and White Mobs Involved

Edited from the article
by George W. Summers,
The *Charleston Daily Mail,*
Sunday Morning, January 23, 1938

In every section of the United States, and in almost every one of the 48 states, there have been lynchings. West Virginia is included among the states where life has been taken as expatiation for atrocious crimes.

But in almost 75 years of the state history of West Virginia there have been so few instances of the enforcement of lynch law that any such action is memorable today. Right here in Charleston, on the very edge of the "Solid South," these two well-established rules - that an innocent victim is not hanged by a mob, and that a Negro mob does not hang a white man - both have been violated.

P. W. Morgan was sheriff of Kanawha County at the time. His deputies included J. T. S. Perry, an old Confederate soldier who had the rank of Colonel, but who throughout the later years of his life was universally known as "Flintlock" Perry. He was known as office deputy sheriff. Silas Morgan was deputy sheriff and jailer.

When P. W. Morgan, the sheriff, learned one evening that plans were being made to bring a mob to the jail for the purpose of hanging the prisoners, he removed them from the jail. When the mob reached the jail soon after dark and the prisoners were not in their cells, they demanded to know where they had been taken. Jailer Silas Morgan and Deputy Perry truthfully asserted they did not know.

A rope was then fastened about the neck of Perry and

was thrown over a branch of a sycamore tree which stood in the courthouse yard, now covered by the present courthouse. Another was put around the neck of Silas Morgan and they were given five minutes to tell where the prisoners were. At this juncture Deputy Perry told the mob that Mrs. Silas Morgan was critically ill at the time and said: "Take me: hang me instead of the jailer, because by so doing you will spare the jailer's sick wife."

The act of self sacrifice on the part of Deputy Sheriff Perry created a profound sensation upon the infuriated mob and the large crowd of bystanders numbering fully 1,500 people. *Only a brave, cool man could have thrown himself into a breach which appeared to be nothing short of death.* Another brave man convinced the quieted mob through Perry's act of courage, to release both "Flintlock" and Morgan.

For nearly two weeks the two white men charged with the taking of two Negro men's lives, were hidden in various places. When quiet was restored, the Negro mob seemed dispersed and the white prisoners were returned to the jail. Without preliminary warning the mob returned, overpowered the officers, and got their men. The entire Negro population had been simultaneously aroused and incensed over the slaying of another respected member of their race. In agreement with the leaders of the white mob, the Negroes would help hang the culprits. Thus, a Negro mob also took a third jailed white man and prepared to hang him.

"With the jail keys forcibly acquired and the prisoners taken from the jail, the two mobs, in the early morning of January 27, left the three men swinging. *This hanging by a Negro mob of the white man may not have been the only instance in the history of the nation, but the writer has been unable to find any other record of such an event.*

When things resumed a more quiet aspect after these horrific events had occurred, Sheriff Morgan said "Perry, the little Rebel, was brave and did his duty well in our late troubles. I shall give Perry the name of 'Flintlock,' meaning in its full appreciation sure and true in all emergencies."

J.T.S. Perry also worked as a printer during his lifetime. He married Fanny Independence Hoffman, born July 4, 1839. She passed away at the very young age of forty-five. Jonathan Theodore Sprigs "Flintlock" Perry was born December 1, 1832. He was of Scotch-Irish and Dutch or German heritage. His ancestors came to America during the "Great Irish Rebellion." When he passed away at the age of 81, July 18, 1913 he was widely remembered as "Flintlock" Perry.

To this day a piece of the sycamore limb over which the rope about Perry's neck was thrown is preserved among the historical treasures of the state bureau of archives and history.

The renowned and respected J.T.S. "Flintlock" Perry.

If someone should ask what is a rescue mission... the statement is penetratingly definitive:

"It is a soul saving place; a place where human wreckage is salvaged...an oasis in a desert of despair; a haven of hope for the homeless and heavyhearted;

"By the grace of God, it is able not only to put a new suit on a man, but much more important, to put a new man in the suit. The mission is a relief society, an employment bureau, a reading and rest room, a restaurant, the poor man's hotel...

"The mission is a place devoted to the reconditioning, the rehabilitating of humans who have been wrecked by the storms of life. The mission is a spiritual awakener, a crime preventer; it is a soul saving and life saving institution..."*

"Our Mission is interdenominational...Jew, Gentile, Catholic or Protestant, are all given a welcome..."

A Mission ..."still motivates those in each generation who unobtrusively fulfill their
MISSION ON MAIN STREET."
by Helga Bender Henry

*Edited version of Ms. Henry's mission statement of the Los Angeles, California, Union Rescue Mission. Joe Perry often quoted passages from her book when speaking to various groups.

Mission on Main Street
by Helga Bender Henry

A glimpse into the history
of the Los Angeles Mission,
established in 1891.
Major George A. Hilton,
Superintendent

Leaving his position as purchasing agent for the Chilean Government, George A. Hilton, born in 1836 in New York City, answered President Lincoln's first call for troops in the Civil War, and enlisted as a private in the 12th regiment, New York Volunteers. The year 1862 found him with the rank of major, but also found him captured and paroled at Harpers Ferry, West Virginia, by "Stonewall Jackson himself."

George Hilton later served fifteen years with the U. S. Treasury Department. He then founded and directed for ten years "one of the largest rescue missions in the world," in Washington, D. C. A mass meeting was held in Los Angeles, "City of the Angels," in 1891, for the purpose of establishing a mission. Major Hilton, possessing a very magnetic personality, was known as a brilliant orator. He answered a call to nightly planning meetings at the Los Angeles YMCA. Those who knew and heard of his abilities and gifts "were convinced of two things: the city must have a rescue mission; Major Hilton must be its Superintendent."

In 1891 he headquartered Los Angeles' first mission in temporary sites, including tent facilities for 3,500 men, within one year. "Two branches were organized, one in Pasadena and one in the 'very slums' of the city on Alameda Street. **The Mission effort was to be undenominational.**"*

One tent was located either at Spring and Second Streets, at First and Los Angeles Streets, or at First and Spring Streets. In its first years the mission seemingly followed a rather nomadic course, but all the time circled the central Main Street area where it was destined to serve the future decades as well.

*All faiths

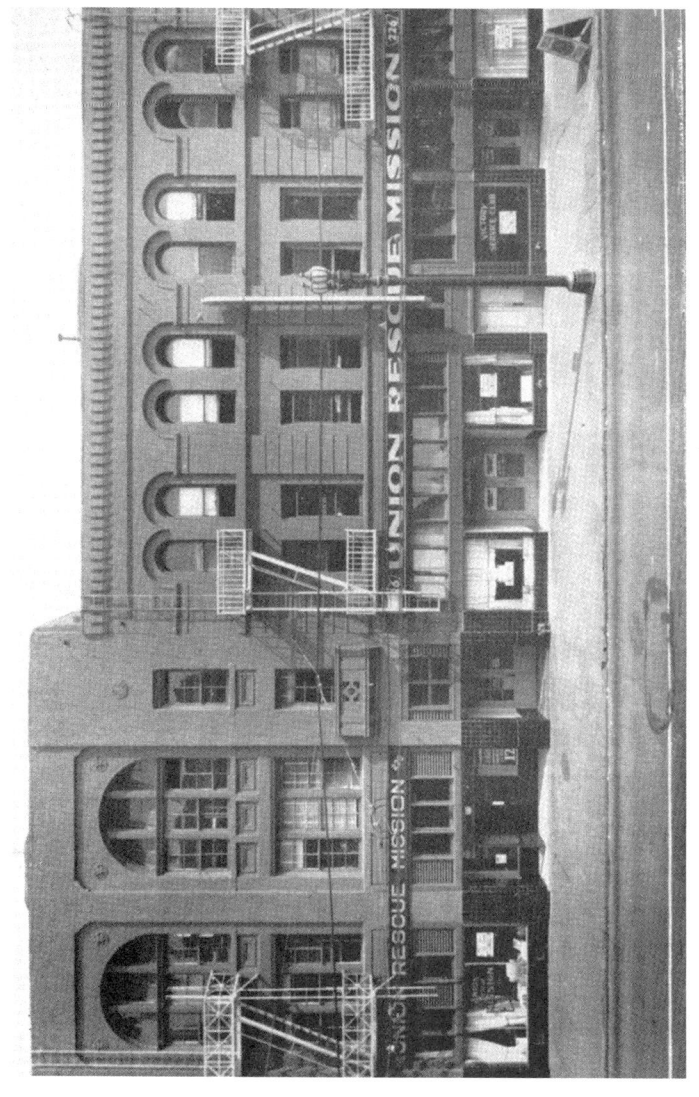

Mission Properties at 226 South Main, Los Angeles

Special Acknowledgments
The Shoemakers

We had often said, "We will never find anyone who will take an interest in the Farm as the Hamptons had for twenty-three years." For a year or more we had not found the right people. Then we found the perfect replacement for the Hamptons.

One day, our daughter Janet remarked that she thought her in-laws might be interested in taking charge of the Farm. Art Shoemaker was employed in Pennsylvania, as well as his wife, Marie. Mr. Guggenheim, our Administrator, wrote to them sending an application. In a short while, they came for a visit to look the situation over. It would mean a much smaller income but they felt it would be rewarding work, thus, they made the decision to come to West Virginia.

The Farm flourished under Art's management and Marie was a fine assistant. Many repairs and improvements were made and several new buildings were built to replace old ones. Art saved the Mission a great deal by doing building, plumbing, and gardening with the help of others. One year the Mission made $10,000 with Art's expertise in beginning a cordwood venture. This was an excellent source of revenue and gave the men additional work.

The grounds are kept in good condition and everyone who visits the Farm is amazed by its beauty. The grounds are also complete for camping and providing food for the Mission. It is wonderful to have vegetables in the spring and summer months, potatoes in the winter.

The Farm has become even more self-supporting by renting the camp to groups when not used by our own young people. We also have farm animals and a few horses for the children to ride.

Beautifully situated three acre lake built with assistance of conservationists- . Purchased in three phases from the Linn, McRobie and Vincent families, the Farm is an extension of the downtown Mission.

Farm superintendent's cottage - Beautiful work by stone mason (who lived at Mission) throughout grounds of Farm. Stones were trucked to Farm from the neighboring families. Mission men were paid fifty cents per wheelbarrow to unload the stones for this archway and buildings.

Robert Guggenheim

Robert Guggenheim was Joe's successor in leading the Union Mission. Joe chose "Bob" because he was a very compassionate man and shared a deep love for people. Joe also felt that the prior Mission experience and administrative skills Bob possessed would help keep the Mission going. Joe knew his successor would need a good sense of humor, another quality Bob revealed.

Bob proved to be a very good leader and was well respected by the community.

Under his leadership the Mission continued to play an integral role in providing housing and food for many, as well as continuing some of the established programs. The youth program continued to flourish, along with the Helping Hand Store and other proven sources of income. Due to ill health Bob retired after many years of faithful service.

*****

Stephen and Delores T. Burger were inspirational to the writer. Delores authored, in 1997, *Women Who Changed the Heart of the City: The Untold Story of the City Rescue Mission Movement.* "Steve" is Executive Director of the Association of Gospel Missions, in N. Kansas City, Missouri.

*****

Former West Virginia Supreme Court Justice **Franklin Cleckley** has been a long-time supporter and friend of Union Mission of Fairmont.

...Special Acknowledgments

Union Mission of Fairmont 2001 Staff

Director - Robert Thompson
Women's Director - Sandy Thompson
Assistant Director/Men's Dir. - Gene Williams
Education Director/Counselor - Joe Peters
Development Director - George Batten
Chaplain - John Rittenhouse
Office Manager/Family Services - Connie Van Gilder
Head Cook - Edith Clossen
Cook - Dorothy Carpenter
Cook - Opal Glaspell
Camp Directors - Jim and Sue Whittacker
Thrift Store Manager - Loretta Loudin
Book Store Manager - Jennifer Wilson
Book Store Clerk - Karen Beavan
Warehouse Manager - Mitch Weaver
Maintenance - Dan Miller
Lee Spencer
Janet Griffin

2001 Board of Directors

Robert Thompson - Dir.
Dr. John Conaway - Pres.
Allen Retton - Vice Pres.
Doug Smith - Secretary
William Goettel - Treasurer
Leslie Brooks
Tracey Beckley
Anthony Horton

Robert "Alan" Ice
James Kettering
Dr. John Manchin
Rick Mullens
Edward Nickolich
Dr. William Phillips
Scott Robertson
Bernard Stalder
Emeritus

Deepest Gratitude to all former Board Members of Union Mission for nearly one half century of dedicated service.

...Special Acknowledgments

The writer is grateful for friends who inspirit my motives through their dedication to children and to the completion of this work.

Jenny Moreno, Socorro Quintana, Monica Arvizu, Robert Ybanez, Rosie Hickey, Harry Southard, Michelle Meyer, Michael and Edith Click, "Nurse Vonda" Dennett, Kathy Taylor, Dick Knisely, "Mr. Bob" Brown, "Mr. Tony" Chavarria, and Terry Lowe. (Tucson)

John Veasey, Maxine Lawson, Tom Hewitt, Betty Gill,* Betty Lou Knapp Nixon, Blake Boggess, D. J.Romino,* Rick and Carol Amos, Diana Christian, Amanda (Oakes) Sabre, Camille (Retton) Knotts, Karen (Kolar) Ouzts, Janet (Marines) Hass, Louise (Meisel) Rankin, Joan Kramer, Randy Spragg, and Nancy (Dollison) Gorman.
John Rittenhouse, David Schepis, and Blaine "Ike" Robinson
are also recognized for research. (East Coast)
The writer recognizes with deepest affection, Ernie, Cecil, and the many unnamed members of the Mission family

* Betty passed away in December, 2001, after long illness.
* D. J. suddenly passed on at fifty-five years of age in April, 2002.

The Union Mission of Fairmont is grateful for the humanitarian support given by West Virginia University throughout the years, especially the dedicated staff of West Virginia University Hospital.

Mr. Tony Caridi, the "Voice of the Mountaineers," was the inspirational keynote speaker in 1999 and 2000 at the Mission's Faith Promise Banquets. His participation has been greatly appreciated and helpful in establishing the "Living Room," a branch of Union Mission in Morgantown, John Rittenhouse, Director.

Prayers and support of the diverse people of St. Francis in the Foothills, Tucson Arizona, David and Susan Wilkinson, and Susan Mullins, have guided me to continue my parent's legacy through this book.

I met Sheryl and Katie Clark at St. Francis. The life of Katie, a beautiful child of nine who gave her allowance to homeless people, was taken in an automobile accident in 1997. This little girl also loved to help make soup for the needy of Tucson.

In her honor the "Katie Clark Memorial Fund for the Homeless" was established. These funds, in conjunction with St. Francis Hunger Ministries, are divided between Casa Maria Soup Kitchen and The Community food Bank of Tucson.

The Reading Seed Program of St. Francis in the Foothills is responsible for assisting many grade school children in need of mentoring. They are commended for their good works in teaching children the love of reading.

For inspiration received from the life of Oprah Winfrey, the writer gives thanks. Oprah's *Angel Network, "Remembering your Spirit,"* and particularly *"Use your Life Series,"* personify the lives of Joe and Fay Perry. Through Oprah (and Friends') formulas for success, empowerment to fulfill my soul mission was achieved...to tell this story, bring this book to reality, and reach higher.

Billy Bob Thornton, actor, director, producer began in the last decade an attempt to popularize "mountain-folk" films. His words were instrumental in keeping my faith to continue writing. He said, *"Regardless of age or circumstance, if you have a goal, never ever give up!"*

This book is also
dedicated in loving memory of

Paul "Mr. Paul" Rutledge
October 25, 1925 - April 4, 2001

Former Crossing Guard
Walter Douglas School
Tucson, Arizona

A man who crossed my path many times, even though we never met. His love for children, like my father's, touched my heart.

The life of "Mr. Paul," World War II veteran, was tragically taken while on duty guarding the lives of school children. He was struck down on a beautiful spring morning by a woman, deeply under the influence, who fled the felony. She was found and charged for this random act of violence.

Index

    Introduction by Fran Perry
    Photo: 1937 Mission opened its doors
13 History and Growth
16 Photo: Perry House and other Mission buildings
17 Photo: Church (former courthouse) landmark
19 Photo: Farm dining lodge
21 **The Joe & Fay Perry Story: Part One**
23 Photo: Joe preferred the woods, nature & library
25 Photo: Fay Summers and her dog, Rex
27 Photo: Joe and Fay Perry
29 **Fay's Stories**
30 Oscar
31 Photo: Oscar and Tom, dining hall, Nov. 1940
37 Photo: Fay Perry
38 Tom Hardy
39 Lawrence
40 Rose, a Story of Tragedy, Yet Love and Compassion
45 Dan
46 The DeLuca Family
48 The Hawkins Family
50 Joe Corporal
51 Margie
55 Bob King
57 Photo: Bob bought Janet her first doll on first Christmas
58 Photo: Carpentry shop for Bob
59 The "Church on Wheels"
60 Martha Nelson Alkire
61 Photo: Mission Musical Messengers music trio
63 Nimrod June Alkire
65 Photo: Men's Building Dorm
66 Frances Hampton
67 Photo: 1947 Youth Group
70 Marsella
72 Dr. Pruitt

73 Photo: Joe Perry, 1940's
74 "Charlie's Mouse"
77 Photo: The Perry Family
81 Photo: Fay Perry 1947
82 Betty Lou
85 Photo: Joe holding Francie football style at 4-H camp
86 The Garcia Family
87 Photo: Janet and Frances
89 Photo: 1950's - Fay Perry - The Substitute Mother
90 "Substitute Mother"
92 Runaways
94 Unwed Mothers - A Home Away From Home
96 Polish John
97 Photo: Francie
98 Mary
99 Photo: Joe Perry in his office
101 Photo: Main building at end of High Level Bridge
104 Irene and Betty
106 The Johnstons
107 Photo: Playground, picnic area enjoyed by youth
108 The Arnolds: Young Parents with a Problem
109 Lucy
111 Fred Holt, "The Umbrella Man"
113 Photo: painting of Fred Holt by Fay Perry
115 Loretta Loudin
117 Photo: Joe Perry at banquet
118 The Richards Family
121 Ken
123 Bunny
125 Charley... "While there is life there is hope."
127 Photo: Joe Perry, later 1950's
128 Charmaine
129 Photo: Charmaine and her sons
131 Joe Duchie
132 George Stake
134 Mr. Peels
135 Dailey: Even a "Possum Rescued"

136 Phillip Chubin
137 Photo: Joe Perry - "there came Phillip with just his shoes on!"
138 The Old Man & A Cup of Cold Water
139 Melina
142 Wilda Michael
143 Photo: Friendly Homes entrance
146 Fay Learns to Drive
147 "Shotgun"
149 Gerald
152 Stanley -- a Polish Emigrant -- Displaced Person
153 Photo: Stanley's Shack on Road to Farmington
154 The "Kidnapper?"
156 Sophie
158 Helen
161 Earl
162 Photo: Joe and Fay at Mission Farms, "County Miracle"
163 Gloria or Glenn?
167 Domingues Family
169 Photo: The Domingues Family
170 Sandra and Mac
175 The Joe and Fay Perry Story, Part Two
177 Photo: Fay Perry and Kesean Stuck
179 Photo: "to rest at his beloved Mission Farm"...
180 The Old Rock House, a Fairmont Mystery
182 Photo: Downtown Mission buildings
183 Photo: Most historically important landmark in downtown Fairmont, red brick former church, acquired by Mission
185 Appendix
186 Footnote to Dan's Story
187 "The Church on Wheels"
188 "Flintlock" Perry - newspaper account of 1876 lynchings
191 A Rescue Mission Defined: excerpt from Mission
192 Main Street by Helga Bender Henry
193 Photo of Los Angeles Mission

194 Special Acknowledgments: The Shoemakers
195 Photos: Lake at the Mission Farm; Farm Cottage
196 Robert Guggenheim
197 Union Mission Staff 2001
197 Board of Directors 2001
198 Special Acknowledgments
200 Second Dedication

2001 is the celebration of the Main Building in its 50th year.

2002 is the 65th Anniversary of the Union Mission.

franjperry_mission@yahoo.com